Feng Shui for Wimps

Simon Brown

Photography by James Duncan

Sterling Publishing Co., Inc.
New York

Created by Lynn Bryan, The BookMaker, London
Design by Mary Staples
Photography by James Duncan
Edited by Anne Hildyard
Props by Maria Brosnan, Denise Eriksen

Library of Congress Cataloging-in-Publication
Data Available

Published by Sterling Publishing Co., Inc.
387 Park Avenue South,
New York, NY 10016

© 2002 Simon Brown

Printed in China
All rights reserved

Sterling ISBN 1-4027-0376-7

Distributed in Canada by
Sterling Publishing
c/o Canadian Manda Group,
One Atlantic Avenue, Suite 105,
Toronto, Ontario, Canada M6K 3EZ

Distributed in Great Britain by Chrysalis
64 Brewery Road, London N7 9NT, England

Distributed in Australia by
Capricorn Link (Australia) Pty Ltd.,
P.O. Box 6651, Baulkham Hills, Sydney,
NSW 2153, Australia.

8

INTRODUCTION

10

THE BASICS

Contents

42

INSTANT
FENG SHUI

68

FIX-ITS

RELATIONSHIPS

92

FIX-ITS

WORK

112

DECORATE IT!

82

FIX-ITS

STRESS

104

FIX-ITS

MONEY

122

CONCLUSION

125

ACKNOWLEDGMENTS

126

INDEX

The reason everyone is still talking about **feng shui** is because *it works* . . .

People have good results with it, they tell their friends, and this keeps popularity alive. Intuitively it **makes sense**. You are bound to *feel good* and *be more successful* in a positive, happy atmosphere. Perhaps the greatest benefit of feng shui is that it makes you **feel more in control of your life.** You can create the atmosphere you want at home and make it easier to feel the way you want to feel. ***You are in the driver's seat!***

Feng Shui originated in China over 4,000 years ago and is part of Chinese history. The idea that "spirit" or "atmosphere of place" has an effect on your well-being is widely accepted today, but in feng shui it has developed into a complex system of theory and practice.

I use a Japanese compass style. For wimps, the underlying concept is that everything in your surroundings, from details on furniture and accessories, to the direction of your front door, can either help you become more successful, or work against you. Once you understand the subtle currents of energy that flow through the universe and your body, you can arrange your environment and your life to enhance emotional and financial success.

Back in the 1980s when I began to work as director of a Community Health Foundation I made it my mission to make feng shui and related subjects accessible to everyday people. This meant using everyday language instead of gobbledygook to explain the subject but, more importantly, taking the principles and applying them in a way that relates to modern-day life. This is the key—to learn and understand the basic principles of feng shui so that that they can be applied to anyone living in any culture. After all, not everyone wants the style and furnishings of their home to replicate one located in central China!

The approach I have taken for you wimps out there is to show you feng shui is a useful tool for your life, rather than a dogma. By the end of this book you'll understand what feng shui is, how it works, and what you can do with it. It is also something you can start using straight away by making simple inexpensive changes to your home. This makes it easy to learn by real life experience so you can see for yourself what kind of results you can expect. And remember, although feng shui has a certain aura of the unfathomably mystical (and yes, it does require a compass and a ruler) it is a flexible philosophy. You don't need a degree in rocket science, nor in interior design. You can just be yourself but take being yourself to the limit for a more successful future.

For many of us pressures of work, raising a family, or having a life of our own means that trying something new like feng shui would need to be made quick and easy, perhaps like viagra for homes! This is probably the best interpretation of feng shui for wimps. Although I have noticed over the years that people who took the wimps' approach eventually brought feng shui into their lives and made it theirs, rather than changing their lives to fit into the subject as some zealots do.

The wimps' approach helps you be in charge, rather than feeling overwhelmed by the concept. Feng shui is only one piece of the jigsaw puzzle of life and not the puzzle itself. This flexible approach means nothing is "wrong," simply good for different things. You make the choice of what you think will help you best. Rather than black and white, it is a rainbow of colors. So don't be afraid to pick up a compass or sketch a floor plan—take the plunge and see how far you can take it.

When I ran the first feng shui courses in the 1980s I was amazed to find that each course was completely full. With what seemed hardly any effort I was able to get feng shui articles in newspapers and before I knew it the largest room in the building would be crowded. Even I used to question people's curiosity for something so "esoteric and obscure" at the time.

When I first used feng shui I was living and renovating an apartment in a desirable area. I later sold the apartment at a time when house prices had fallen by 20 percent and I was amazed to find my home had actually increased in value to such an extent that it more than covered the cost of the renovations.

Simultaneously, the apartment above mine was also for sale. Structurally, and in size, it was almost identical to mine. My neighbors were desperate to sell the apartment, yet all their efforts seemed in vain. While I could hardly keep potential customers away. The people who bought my home fell in love with the atmosphere of the place. In the end, the neighbors sold their apartment for a much lower price. This convinced me that feng shui was more than just an interesting Chinese philosophy.

The more I played around with feng shui the more I discovered the power behind it. I have four boys; one of the first experiments was to change their sleeping position to see if it would help them sleep better. Children are good "guinea pigs" when it comes to feng shui, as it could not be a placebo for them. Sleeping with the top of their heads pointing north certainly helped them get to sleep and we were woken less in the middle of the night with one of them wanting a cuddle. However, north is a little too quiet energy for young people. In the end we chose east as this seemed to make it easier for them to get up early and set off for school full of energy. Or was I just missing those cuddles?!

In 1993 I became a full-time feng shui consultant with the help of my Japanese teacher and found myself working with fascinating people from all walks of life. To name a few: dj and pop star Boy George, Lorenzo Poccianti, the owner of an Italian castle, and large companies like The Body Shop, and British Airways. My computer is now loaded with thousands of clients' reports and drawings. One of the most wonderful things about my job is that many of my clients have become friends—two birds with one stone!

The question I get asked the most by people inquiring about a consultation is what results they can expect. Since I have been trying to keep in contact with my clients over the years I believe I have a good knowledge and feel for what can happen when you use feng shui. Nearly everyone feels more relaxed at home and has a greater awareness of the atmosphere in their home. Most people find they feel better and as a result can put more effort into getting what they want out of life and some people have the most incredible results that surprise me as much as them.

I used to dread social occasions when the standard question "and what do you do for living?" would surface in conversation. With almost any other job, I would have not needed a job description. Everlastingly I had to explain rather than just say what I did. These days the question that follows the one about my job is most likely to be: Is it true that I should/should not have so and so in my kitchen? Or, my husband can't sleep, which way should he face?

Back then some people were already saying feng shui was a fad and would soon be over and yet, years later, I am still as busy as ever.

Feng Shui is the art of setting up your home so you feel good and can do more with your life. This section explains how it works, and how to apply these ancient principles to your modern lifestyle.

The

Basics

You and your home

You are your home may be an overstatement, yet there is an element of truth about it. When you spend a lot of time in one place you become immersed in the atmosphere of that space, so you naturally take on something of its character.

Of course, this also works the other way around and we can change the atmosphere of our home by the way we decorate it, and as we bring energy into the home, the atmosphere will take on elements of our individual personality. As an exercise, I went around to people's homes to see how much I could find out about them just by looking at their living space. I was amazed at how

Fill your home with things that give you a lift and a buzz. Feel proud of your home!

accurate I could be. It was even possible to pick up information on their relationships, and I could tell who tended to "rule" the home. We all do this intuitively, and when we go into someone's home for the first time, we pick up signals, which will color our impression of the host.

When you walk into a room just after someone has had an argument, you can pick up on the atmosphere. Then, it takes some time to feel calm yourself. In feng shui you are constantly coloring the atmosphere of your home by the thoughts and emotions you have while you are there. All this will make you and your home a partnership that can

work against you, or actually help you succeed in life. The idea of feng shui is to know what you want to do with your life, and then create the atmosphere at home to help you do it.

Make a list of anything big or small, general or specific that would help. When I do this exercise with students, they state more spiritual goals, but there is nothing wrong with including a love life, fast cars, or vacations. Finally, you need to decide what it is you need to change about yourself to help make it happen. For example, you might need to be more patient, assertive, or expressive. This will become your guide for creating the launch pad for a new life.

TRY THIS

If you have trouble knowing what you want, try this exercise. Lie down or sit in a comfy chair, breathe deeply and relax. Imagine you are at the end of your life taking your last breath yet you feel very content, complete, and satisfied. You can feel yourself leaving your body and moving on, and you are looking forward to a new experience. Once you are really good at getting those feelings, start to think about what you have to do between now and then to ensure you feel content at the end of your life.

Seeing decorating accessories you chose for their style and energy brings a boost to your self-esteem every time you look at them when you come home.

Glossary

There are many and various terms people use when talking about and using feng shui. Here are a few of the more important terms, with an explanation of their meaning.

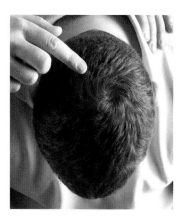

FENG SHUI

Feng shui literally translates to wind and water. The way these elements move around our planet are much the same as the flow of feng shui energy. They both form a connection with the outside world and our bodies. Our bodies are 70 percent water, and the water inside us is constantly being replenished by fresh water outside in a similar way that we take in oxygen from the air. These are vital links to our environment—without either we soon die. Feng shui is based on the same idea but focuses on an energy that carries information about us and constantly blends and updates it with energy from the world around us.

CHI ENERGY

Chi energy is a subtle electromagnetic energy that flows through everything we know, passing on information from one entity to another. It is as though everything is linked by an invisible network so that we influence, and are influenced by, everything we know. In the human body chi energy carries our thoughts, ideas, and emotions. This energy extends beyond our bodies enveloping us inside our own chi energy field. This can be seen using a process called Kirlian photography. It is easy to be influenced by the atmosphere of a home and this is why we feel different in different places.

CHAKRAS

The chakras are seven points along the body where your chi energy is particularly active. These are the spiral at the top of your head, the area between your eyebrows, your throat, between your nipples, your stomach, just below your navel, and the base of your spine. These areas are often used in healing to create a more healthy flow of chi energy around your body.

MERIDIANS

These are paths that carry chi energy around your body. They feed smaller branches until your chi reaches every cell in your body. This means that every thought and emotion will touch every cell and over the long term it can affect your physical body. The reverse is also true so the condition of your cells and body changes the way your energy flows. You may have noticed that it is very hard to remain angry if you breathe slowly and stretch out, or get depressed if you are in the middle of a vigorous exercise. The way you use your body also changes the way chi energy flows and that changes the way you think and feel.

YIN AND YANG

The literal translation is that yin represents the shady side of the mountain and yang the sunny side. However, yin and yang can be used to describe anything. Something will always be more yin or yang than something else. Yin or yang can be applied to the decoration of your home, the food you eat, the clothes you wear, or any of your activities. Generally, yang refers to anything that makes you active, energetic, quick, alert, focused, precise, aggressive, assertive, or tense. Yin describes everything that helps you relax, slow down, open your mind, be creative, stimulate your imagination, be flexible and easygoing, look at the bigger picture, and be receptive.

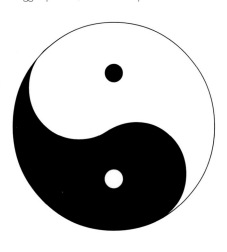

FIVE ELEMENTS

These are five different kinds of chi energy represented by the elements tree, fire, soil, metal, and water. Each energy is associated with a time of day and season. This is the easiest way to get a feel for what the energy is. Imagine being out in nature at the same time of day and year.

Tree: sunrise and spring. Fire: midday and summer. Soil: afternoon and summer changing to autumn. Metal: sunset and autumn. Water: midnight and winter.

The most important aspect is the way they relate to each other. This forms the basis of working out why there might be problem areas in a home, and how to solve them.

FIVE ANIMALS

The five animals also relate to five energies; they are positioned around your body and always take the same position. The energy in front of you is represented by the phoenix, to your right by the tiger, to your rear by the tortoise, to your left the dragon, and the center by the snake.

EIGHT DIRECTIONS

The eight directions are used to build up a character for the energy found in each of the directions. So for example the energy of the east will have the character of the sunrise, the morning, and spring. This might be a helpful energy to absorb into your own chi energy field if you want that get up and go feeling. Let's make it happen anyway!

Conversely the sunset energy of the west is associated with the autumn harvest time and the end of the day. This would be better for completing things properly or perhaps harvesting the rewards of your hard work. Once you know what of each of the eight directions has to offer, you can use feng shui to bring more of that energy into your being.

TRIGRAMS

The trigrams are made of three lines. Broken lines are more yin and solid lines are more yang. There are eight arrangements of these lines and each is linked to one of the eight directions.

MAGIC SQUARE

Feng shui is based on Fu Hsi's magic square. The numbers one to nine are arranged so any three in a straight line always add up to fifteen. Each number is either more yin or yang, has a five element, and a trigram. This grid is laid over your house plan to see the flow of energy there.

4	9	2
3	5	7
8	1	6

Chi energy

We usually think of ourselves as being contained within our skin, however, in feng shui we are much bigger than that. We are essentially emotional beings and in feng shui the energy of our thoughts, ideas, and emotions is carried by what is known as chi energy.

Sitting back to back can merge energy fields. Relax as much as you can and let your mind wander. See what kind of thoughts and emotions float in. Talk to your partner after the experience to see if you both had the same kind of feelings and thoughts.

This means that our thoughts and emotions actually continue outside our bodies. For this reason they can be influenced by outside forces and you will find that the atmosphere in certain buildings will make you think and feel differently.

How do we know it exists? You may have had the experience of feeling someone behind you and turning around to see if someone is there. This would be an example of your chi energy field interacting with someone else's. In a similar way you will probably notice that you feel comfortable with certain people or in some places. This means your chi is reacting harmoniously with your surroundings and it is being calmed by the energy around you. On other occasions people or a special space may be particularly stimulating for you and help inspire you to new ideas. Choosing the best environment for what you want to do is part of the secret of being able to do more with less effort.

At times I notice my chi energy flows very easily with that of other people. It feels like we are on the same wavelength and it is easy to exchange ideas and feelings. The energy of the interaction carries much more than the words alone. You can try an interesting exercise to develop these feelings. Sit back to back with someone. Your energy fields will now be immersed in each other's. Try to relax as much as you can and let your mind wander. See what kind of thoughts and emotions float in. When you are active, or concentrating, you will tend to radiate more chi energy than you take in, so the more relaxed and empty you are, the more receptive you will be. After a while, discuss the experience with the other person and see if you influenced each other.

As well as being influenced by other people, our chi energy, and, therefore, thoughts and feelings, will be influenced by the chi energy of the food we eat, our environment, and buildings we live in. Feng shui primarily focuses on the way the atmosphere in buildings influences the way we feel.

Acupuncture and shiatsu work on the principle that some of your chi energy is channeled into paths as it flows around your body. These are known as meridians and along each meridian there are acupressure points where your chi energy can be influenced more easily.

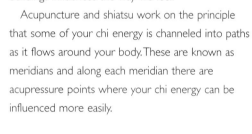

Vibes at home

Chi energy around your home will enter and influence the energy inside. If you live in a quiet rural area more of this energy will enter your home. Someone living near a busy street in a city will absorb more of that energy.

Anybody home?
Each time you pass through a doorway your energy field stirs up the energy there, creating a stronger flow.

Chi energy will flow along the easiest path such as doors and windows. There can be strong currents of chi energy around doors, since this path of chi energy is stirred up each time anyone enters, or leaves, through the door. Your own chi energy field pushes and drags energy along with it, causing the chi energy to be more active in those areas. In some cases, this can lead to a strong current of energy that makes the home hard to relax in. For example, this happens when several doors are in a straight line.

The position and size of doors and windows will make a difference to the flow of energy. The larger the opening, the easier and quicker energy can flow toward an active space.

Openings that face a sunny direction will bring in more lively, fiery chi energy, creating a stimulating atmosphere.

The energy moving through the doors and windows will generate a horizontal flow of chi. Some of the earth's energy will rise vertically through the floor and energy from space will enter through the ceiling. Stairs will add to this a vertical flow of energy.

Homes with low ceilings and lots of windows on both sides will have a greater horizontal flow of energy. This is more common in rooms closer to the ground, than in loft apartments. The effect of this horizontal flow is energy passes more easily from one person to the next, making it ideal for being social and interactive. Spaces with high ceilings, those set on the side of a hill or a mountain, or narrow spaces can have a more vertical flow of energy. This is most typical in loft apartments where the pointed ceiling also encourages energy to flow vertically. It is common to feel individualistic in these atmospheres.

This room, with its tall ceilings and strong vertical lines has an up atmosphere, and is an excellent example of tree energy.

Sharp corners that point into a room will often have a strong, piercing flow of energy. If the corner points to your bed, or a chair you like to sit in, there is a risk you will find it hard to sleep well.

The people living in a home will also influence the atmosphere. Buying a home from a couple who have had an acrimonious divorce or where there was great unhappiness, can risk you being submersed in some of that energy yourself for a while. A home in which you feel happy and that coincides with a successful period of your life will pick up some of that energy.

Yin and yang

With yin and yang, you can see how you interact with everything around you. This concept becomes valuable when deciding what kind of environment would suit you best. It also helps you find out more about yourself, and what will make you successful.

BEING NATURALLY YIN

THE PRINCIPLE

Yin and yang describe chi energy. Yin is slow, dispersed, and flexible. Passive. Yang is fast, piercing, concentrated, and active. By diagnosing whether you are more yin (passive) or yang (active), you can use the opposite to bring a better balance to yourself.

We can be born more yang or yin. However, all of life's experiences can later add to this natural state. At the time of the full moon, for example, people become more yang; they are more active and more sociable. However, at the time of the new moon, they become more relaxed, calm, and spiritual.

When I have a busy schedule, I make myself more yang-focused and active by eating more fish, grains, and root vegetables, and by exercising and getting up early. When the busy period is over, and I need to unwind, I go for more yin things like salads, fruit, and juices; I stretch my body more, and have a massage to relax.

If you are too yin or yang you may experience problems or discomforts. If too yang, you may become tense and impatient. This is usually accompanied by a stiff neck and shoulders. If you become too yin you may feel tired, lethargic, and sometimes depressed.

The easiest way to get out of being too yang is to make yourself more yin. For instance, travel to the country, spend more time on your own, or with a close friend, and watch comedies, or read an amusing book.

To be more yang, exercise more, be around stimulating people, and immerse yourself in work.

YIN CHARACTERISTICS

Someone who is constitutionally yin generally has an oval-shaped face, a leaner frame, and long fingers and slender toes. Large eyes, full lips, and fleshy cheeks will further indicate that this person is more yin. Someone who blinks more often and finds it harder to make eye contact will usually be more yin. These qualities include being creative, imaginative, and being sensitive to the emotions of those around them, and what's happening in the world at large. This type of person can also be flexible, easygoing, and gentle in their nature. They enjoy watching television, meditating, and reading a book.

Anyone who is naturally more yin can slip into becoming too yin more frequently than getting too yang. It could be a mistake to let someone like this become lethargic, withdrawn, or develop a victim mentality.

Create a more yin appearance by wearing loose, comfortable clothes. Pastel colors—in particular blue, pink, or green—help you feel more relaxed. Wooden beads, a rope bracelet, and a scarf will reinforce this effect. Longer hair, pale make-up, and pastel-colored ribbons in your hair (for females) can strengthen a yin image.

BEING NATURALLY YANG

YANG CHARACTERISTICS

Someone who is inherently more yang will have a rounder face, be stockier, shorter, and look solid. This person will be particularly yang if he or she has smaller eyes, thin lips, and a well-developed jaw line.

These people find it easy to be focused, alert, and precise. They enjoy being active and thrive on a dynamic lifestyle. They are competitive, ambitious, and can get angry. They're also quick-thinking, logical, and precise.

Such a person can find they drift into becoming too yang more easily than going through periods of being yin. They need to be careful of overworking, taking life too seriously, and setting too high standards both for themselves and those around them.

To look more yang, wear bright colors, clothes with sharp lines, and made of shiny materials such as leather. Also wear metal accessories and sunglasses.

Short-cropped hair, no hair, or unshaven stubble creates a stronger yang appearance. Brightly colored make-up (for women) and body-piercing (for either sex) creates a strong yang accent.

ARE YOU YIN OR YANG?

✔ One of the easiest ways to check whether you are more yin or yang on a daily basis is to compare yourself with other people.

✔ When you find other people generally too slow, unreliable, and indecisive, plus notice you are getting irritable or frustrated with them, you are too yang. Conversely, when it is obvious the people around you are getting annoyed because you feel like taking it easy, or when you cannot be bothered to make an effort, and others appear tense and uptight, it is clear that you are too yin.

✔ Watch how you behave and how people react to you over a period of time to work out which type you think you might be. Try it with your friends, too.

KEY POINTS

● Yang food includes salt, meat, eggs, fish and grains. Yin food includes salads, fruit, liquids, ice cream, and sugar.

● Yang exercise includes boxing, karate, and tennis. Yin exercise includes stretching, yoga, and Tai Chi.

● Yang mental activities include financial accounting, studying, and playing chess.

● Yin mental activities include painting, reading, and chatting.

Yin and yang at home

The way chi energy flows in your home will make a difference to the way you feel there. It is interesting to look at the different ways chi energy flows and how this will affect you in terms of yin and yang.

In an open, spacious home with hard surfaces, such as stone floors and metal furniture, chi energy will flow much faster, making the rooms feel livelier and more yang. Here it would be easier to feel active and stimulated (yang) but the atmosphere would make it harder to relax (yin). This would be similar to the sensation of being on a mountain where the energy moves freely and quickly. It is excellent for getting new ideas, clearing your mind, and feeling inspired.

In a home that has smaller rooms, which is well-furnished, and has many soft surfaces, such as carpets, curtains, cushions, and rugs, the energy will move more slowly and be more yin. In this atmosphere it is easier to relax, be settled, and feel comfortable; all the characteristics of feeling more yin. This atmosphere is similar to what you'd feel sitting among bushes and trees, next to a slow-moving river.

Being close to the floor helps you be more yin and relaxed. Lie on the floor, sit on large, soft cushions, or flop into a low, comfortable chair when you feel uptight.

In some places, the energy can become squashed, making it much more yang and intense. This happens where lots of people pass through a small entrance, or in a corridor. These are potentially stressful atmospheres, plus this harmful energy can carry on into rooms nearby.

The opposite is true of a room with little light, such as a basement apartment, where the energy becomes too dispersed and yin. In this situation, it is easier to feel too yin, sometimes leading to depression, and a loss of vitality.

In this case, add large and small mirrors, paint the room white or off-white or cream, adding touches of yellow, red, or any bright color. Play a track or two of lively music, to speed up the energy.

A clever lighting scheme using uplighters, especially in or near dark corners, adds more positive energy in situations like this, too.

Sitting on a tall chair or stool makes it easier to feel more yang. Try doing this when you want to concentrate, and feel more focused.

Five elements at play

The five elements are interesting in terms of seeing how chi energies interact with each other as they are built on a model in which energies can feed, calm, or even destroy each other. The model is used primarily to try and see where there are possible conflicts of energy at home and to then provide solutions.

Each of the five types of chi energy are similar to the atmosphere you would experience at a certain time of day, and in a specific season.

In addition to this they are associated with natural elements found in nature, materials you might find in your home, different directions within your home, and with shapes and colors. Each of the five energies is known by one of the elements—tree (wood), fire, soil, metal, and water.

The elements are arranged in a circle, with water at the bottom and fire at the top. This relates to the movement of the sun where it comes up in the east—tree, reaches its highest point in the south— fire, and sets in the west—metal.

Soil describes the afternoon sun descending, and water describes the night. Similarly, you can follow the seasons by moving around the circle. Water is winter, tree is springtime, fire is summer, soil is summer changing to fall, and metal is fall.

Water, tree, fire, soil, and metal are just different names to describe the atmosphere you experience at different times of the day and the year.

Tree energy is generally up, active, and full of hope, like we might feel on a sunny, spring morning. Fire is more outward, expressive and colorful, similar to the feelings we could have in the middle of a hot summer's day. Soil resembles the settled, secure, and established energy at the end of a summer's afternoon. Metal describes energy moving inward, becoming concentrated and contained. Think of gathering the fall harvest and watching a red sunset; it is all about bringing things into your life and feeling content.

Water relates to going with the flow, being flexible, and deep regeneration. Think of being outdoors, surrounded by nature, in the middle of the night in midwinter.

When all these five energies are present in your chi energy field they work in perfect harmony, feeding and calming each other. Look at the chart and you will see that water feeds tree, tree feeds fire, and so on. At the same time, tree calms water, fire calms tree, and carries on around the circle.

For example, if you have too much fire energy and feel explosive, more soil energy—in the form of being with someone who is down-to-earth and caring, or doing something practical—will help calm you down. If you did not have enough fire energy and felt withdrawn, more tree energy—exercise, sports, and adventure—will feed the fire energy inside you and help you feel more sociable again.

You can also feed or calm these energies within yourself by changing the atmosphere in your home. Simply use the preceding element in the part of your home occupied by the element you want more of. To increase the water energy of the north, put a metal wind chime there. Makes sure it chimes daily. To increase the tree energy of the east, place a water feature in the east part of your home. Tall plants in the south part will feed the fire energy there. Candles in the center or southwest will feed the local soil energy. Yellow flowers in a clay container will feed the metal energy of the west.

Conversely, you can calm each energy by using the following element, and placing something with that energy in the part that relates to the energy you want to calm.

DEALING WITH A DEFICIENCY

When one of the five elements is deficient, the preceding energy can destroy the following energy. For example, if tree energy is deficient, water chi energy would be destructive to fire chi energy. Think of having a late winter—water—a short spring— tree—and then summer. The late frost and cold weather would be destructive to the summer crops.

In a home, a similar scenario could occur where you have a bathroom in the southern part of your home. The water energy of the bathroom would then be mixed in with the fire energy of the south. If some tree energy was present, this would not be a potential problem. However, if tree energy was not present, the water energy could be destructive to the local fire energy, resulting in you not feeling very expressive, outgoing, or social.

Common situations where two types of chi energy enter into a destructive relationship concern fire or water. In reality, it means energy associated with boilers, fireplaces, stoves, and ovens for fire energy; and bathrooms, toilets, kitchen sinks, washing machines, and dishwashers for water energy.

The remedy for a situation where one of the energies is deficient, leaving two energies in conflict, is to simply add more of the deficient energy.

So in the example of the bathroom in the south part of your home, you add more tree chi energy to restore a harmonious relationship between water, tree, and fire.

Confused at this stage and want to wimp out? Stay with it! Follow the simple guidelines over the page and your life will improve!

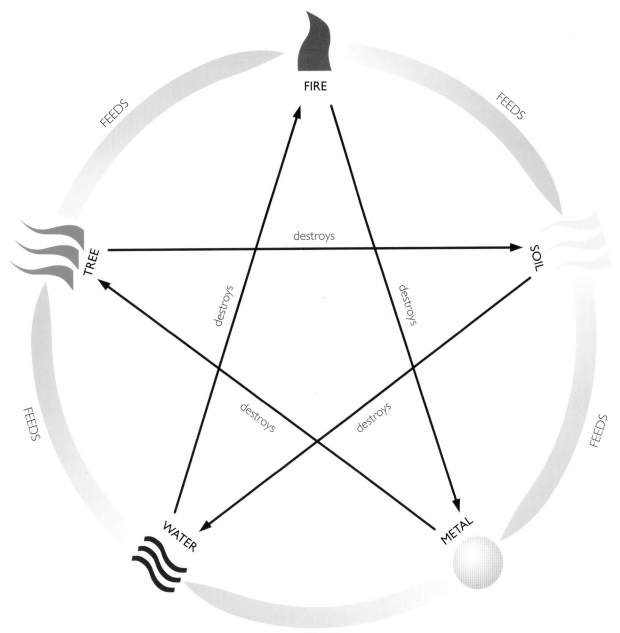

Answers for wimps!

Here are just some of the typical situations where problems can occur, with my suggested solutions. Consider your concerns, read through these problems, look at the suggestions, and then try the solution. Take note, over a few weeks, of the consequences. You just might be surprised.

FEELING WITHDRAWN, LONELY, AND IGNORED?

✔ Check if you have a bathroom, toilet, utility room, water feature, or kitchen sink in the south part of your home.

The remedy: put more tree chi energy there in the form of plants, timber flooring, wooden furniture, or wooden objects. Use the color green.

FIND IT HARD TO MAINTAIN LONG-TERM RELATIONSHIPS, SAVE MONEY, OR GO WITH THE FLOW?

✔ Check if you have a bathroom, toilet, utility room, water feature, or kitchen sink in the southwest part of your home.

The remedy: put more metal chi energy there in the form of metal objects, metal fittings, or hard stone flooring. Use the color light gray.

TREE
- Spring / morning
- Rising
- Green / vertical / wood, wicker, cork
- Tall plants
- Feed with water features.
- Calm with candles.

FIRE
- Summer / midday
- Outward
- Red / lights / pointed
- Candles
- Feed with plants.
- Calm with charcoal.

SOIL
- Summer-autumn / afternoon
- Descending
- Yellow / horizontal / clay, soft stone, fabric, charcoal
- Candles
- Feed with candles.
- Calm with metal objects.

UNMOTIVATED, INFLEXIBLE, OR UNABLE TO KEEP HEALTHY?

✔ Check if you have a bathroom, toilet, utility room, water feature, or kitchen sink in the northeast part of your home.

The remedy: put more metal chi energy there in the form of metal objects, metal fittings, or hard stone flooring. Use the color light gray.

WONDERING WHY YOU CANNOT FIND THAT ROMANTIC FEELING, GET MONEY IN THE BANK, OR FEEL CONTENT?

✔ Check if you have a fireplace, stove, boiler, or oven in the west part of your home.

The remedy: put more soil chi energy there in the form of charcoal in a clay pot, yellow flowers in a clay container, or add a soft stone floor. Use the color yellow.

FEEL DISORGANIZED, OUT OF CONTROL, OR LACK RESPECT?

✔ Check to see if you have a fireplace, stove, boiler, or oven in the northwest part of your home.

The remedy: put more soil chi energy there in the form of charcoal in a clay pot, yellow flowers in a clay container, or add a soft stone floor. Use the color yellow.

SUFFERING FROM LOW SEXUAL VITALITY, DECREASED HEALING POWERS, OR POOR SLEEP?

✔ Check to see if you have a bathroom, toilet, utility room, water feature, or kitchen sink in the north part of your home.

The remedy: put more tree chi energy there in the form of plants, timber flooring, wooden furniture, or wooden objects. Use the color green.

METAL
- Autumn / sunset
- Inward
- Silver / circles / metal, hard stone
- Clocks
- Feed with yellow flowers in clay container.
- Calm with water and glass.

WATER
- Winter / midnight
- Flowing
- Translucent or glossy black or blue / wavy / glass
- Crystal
- Feed with a metal wind chime.
- Calm with plants.

Five animals

The five animals are simply an image to describe the energy around you, and how to work out the best place to sit in both business and social situations. Be smart—arrive early and always take up the most powerful place. Take your positions!

Our chi energy field is most comfortable when it is allowed to take up its natural shape. In feng shui the five animals describe an individual's shape. Each animal describes the way energy flows and takes up a position around your body.

The phoenix always takes up a position in front of you. The tiger is located to your right, with the tortoise at your rear. The dragon sits to your left, and the snake to your center.

The phoenix symbolizes your energy flying forward and spreading out. It is therefore essential that you have plenty of open space in front of you. The tortoise represents your hard, protective shell and you need something solid and secure behind you. The dragon describes energy moving up next to you, and the tiger is symbolic of the defensive energy to your right. Think of the dragon taking a more offensive role and the tiger a more protective role. The snake is within you, orchestrating the four animals around you. The animals always stay in the same positions around you, regardless of which way you are facing.

This way of looking at your energy field is most useful when considering where to position yourself within a room. Ideally, the wall should be behind you, representing the tortoise, with as much open space in front of you as possible to symbolize the phoenix. This space is the room and, where possible, the door and windows. Some kind of partial enclosure to your right would help provide energy for the tiger. This could be a low table. A plant to your left would encourage the upward energy of the dragon.

With this position in mind you can immediately spot the best chair in any café, restaurant, or meeting room. I notice that, when they have a choice, people will intuitively take up the best position in a hotel lobby or public space. Having taught my children

Backs to the wall!
Sitting in a café with
the wall behind you and
everything in front of
you puts you in the
seat of power.

these principles there is always an ungainly rush to get the best seat when we go out. There is nothing worse than sitting with your back to the door or to a busy room.

Arrange your rooms at home so you benefit from the energy of the animals. Try sitting as far from the door as possible, so you face into the room and have a good view of the window. You do not need to face the door or window, just ensure you have a good view of it. Place a chair there and sit on it for a while. You should feel a greater sense of power, almost as though you are in control of the room. Everything is laid out in front of you.

As a consultant, I encounter people whose desks are right against a wall. In that situation, everything is behind them and the wall constricts their energy in front of

them. In this scenario, it is much harder to think of big ideas, to express yourself freely, and feel like you are moving forward in life. What is worse, you have the distraction of things going on behind you, especially if you work in a busy office.

If you cannot take the ideal position, try to re-create it using various objects. For example, a tall plant, a piece of furniture, or a screen can become the protective tortoise behind your back. A mirror helps you see what is happening behind you, or gives you a view of the door. Lower plants or low furniture help provide the energies of the dragon and tiger.

Set up your workspace so you can see people as they approach you, and easily make eye contact. This is good for team work and being included in projects.

Lost in space?

The eight directions will lead you wherever you want to go. Around you are different kinds of chi energy. By turning to your right or left, you will face a different flavor of chi energy. The energy is different because of the way the sun affects our planet, the earth's magnetic field, and the forces of other planets. This means you can absorb more of one specific energy into your own energy field, taking on more of its characteristics. The easiest way to do this is to sleep with the top of your head pointing in the direction that has the energy of which you need more.

In this system, the energies are divided into the four points of the compass, north, east, south, and west and the four directions in between. The energy of each direction is associated with a time of day, season, five element, and trigram. The trigrams are a series of three parallel lines, which are either solid or broken. The solid lines are yang and the broken lines yin. The trigrams are linked to a family member and those that share a common five element have their own unique symbol from nature.

Read through the description for each direction below and see if any sound like something you need more of. The colors in this system are slightly different from the ones in the five elements. The numbers refer to their position in the magic square.

East–enthusiastic   **Southeast**–creative   **South**–expressive   **Southwest**–caring   **West**–playful

 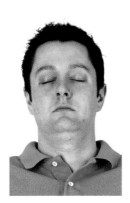 

Northwest–intuitive   **North**–peaceful   **Northeast**–determined

Each of the eight directions is associated with a certain type of energy (see following pages). Here are examples of eight different emotions associated with each direction. Absorbing more of each direction's energy will make it easier to access those emotions.

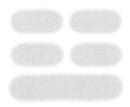

EAST

Trigram	Yin / Yin / Yang
Five Element	Tree
Symbol	Thunder
Family Member	Eldest son
Magic square no.	3
Color	A bright green, similar to a new leaf
Time	Morning—sunrise
Season	Spring

Helpful for being enthusiastic, confident, and assertive. Can increase the risk of frustration and anger. Increases the desire to start new projects, be alert, focus on details, get things right, analyze, be precise, and concentrate. The symbol of thunder gives this energy a loud, forceful edge, which is helpful for going out and making things happen. It is a useful direction if you want to wake up and get up earlier.

SOUTHEAST

Trigram	Yang / Yang / Yin
Five Element	Tree
Symbol	Wind
Family Member	Eldest daughter
Magic square no.	4
Color	The same dark green as a mature leaf and a sky blue
Time	Midmorning—sun rising in the sky
Season	Spring changing to summer

Helpful for being persistent, sensitive, and feeling positive. Can increase the risk of feeling irritable and impatient. Increases the desire to be creative, be imaginative, generate new ideas, seek harmony, communicate, and spread ideas. The symbol of wind makes it ideal for spreading ideas in a similar way that wind spreads seeds. As it relates to the morning and spring, it is a good energy to make progress in life, although more harmoniously than thunder. The progress you make with this energy is also associated with future prosperity.

SOUTH

Trigram	Yang / Yin / Yang
Five Element	Fire
Symbol	Fire
Family Member	Middle daughter
Magic square no.	9
Color	A fiery, bright reddish purple
Time	Midday—sun at highest point
Season	Midsummer

Good for being passionate, excited, proud, generous, flamboyant, and dramatic. Can also lead to feeling self-centered, stressed, and hysterical. Increases the desire to be expressive, get noticed, be social, be outgoing, be spontaneous, lead fashions, and be quick minded. This fiery chi energy is bright, colorful, and radiates energy.

SOUTHWEST

Trigram	Yin / Yin / Yin
Five Element	Soil
Symbol	Earth
Family Member	Mother
Magic square no.	2
Color	Matte black or brown similar to charcoal or rich soil
Time	Afternoon—sun moving down in the sky
Season	Summer changing to fall

Good for being caring, patient, and sympathetic. Can risk feeling dependent and jealous. Increases the desire to be practical, down-to-earth, consolidate, add quality, form long-term relationships, and be secure. The late summer represents the time of year when fruits and vegetables have stopped growing and are ripening. It is therefore the ideal energy for improving the quality of whatever you do. The settling soil energy is helpful for deepening relationships with friends, lovers, or family.

WEST

Trigram	Yin / Yang / Yang
Five Element	Metal
Symbol	Lake
Family Member	Youngest daughter
Magic square no.	7
Color	This is the color of the sunset, including a rusty red, maroon, and pink
Time	Early evening—sunset
Season	Fall

Good for being romantic, content, and playful but can lead to feeling depressed and pessimistic. Increases the desire to enjoy the pleasures of life, be wealthy, form new relationships, be stylish, and complete projects. West is associated with the harvest time and the end of the day, making this chi energy ideal for bringing things to a profitable conclusion. The youngest daughter is associated with being playful, seeking fun, and enjoying the pleasures of life.

NORTHWEST

Trigram	Yang / Yang / Yang
Five Element	Metal
Symbol	Heaven
Family Member	Father
Magic square no.	6
Color	Silver gray or off-white, the color of metal
Time	Late evening—dusk
Season	Fall changing to winter

Good for being in charge, dignified, and responsible. In excess, risks being authoritarian and arrogant. Increases the desire to feel in control, organize, plan ahead, be respected, and have integrity. This is the most yang trigram; three solid lines and representing the father. The symbol of heaven means it is helpful for greater wisdom and clearer intuition. The energy represents experience and maturity, making it is easier to win people's trust, command respect, and be, or find, a mentor.

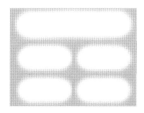

NORTH

Trigram	Yin / Yang / Yin
Five Element	Water
Symbol	Water
Family Member	Middle son
Magic square no.	1
Color	Cream, ideally with a high-gloss finish or a clear varnish, or other translucent finishes
Time	Night—darkness
Season	Midwinter

Good for being sexual, spiritual, and independent, although also risks feeling isolated and aloof. Increases the desire to be flexible, find peace, study, develop oneself, improve health, be objective, and be different. This energy is useful for having original ideas without being influenced by other people. It is ideal for conception and improving your sex life. Your health, ability to heal yourself, and vitality are particularly influenced by this chi energy. It's also helpful if you have trouble sleeping.

NORTHEAST

Trigram	Yang / Yin / Yin
Five Element	Soil
Symbol	Mountain
Family Member	Youngest son
Magic square no.	8
Color	A brilliant white rather like a snow-peaked mountain
Time	Early morning, first haze of light
Season	Winter changing to spring

Good for being motivated, driven, and outgoing, however can also encourage you to be greedy and shrewd. Increases the desire to seize opportunities, win, compete, learn, be decisive, clear minded and adventurous. The energy is sharp, piercing and quick to change, making it good for striking a deal and trading. It is similar to a strong cold northeasterly wind and therefore good for clearing your mind, helping you be more decisive, and for thinking of a new direction in life.

CENTER

Trigram	None
Five Element	Soil
Symbol	None
Family Member	None
Magic square no.	5
Color	Yellow or orange
Time	None
Season	None

This energy links all the eight directions. It does not have a specific trigram, time, or season, but can be said to represent them all. As such, it is an energy that can help you become the center of attention and attract people to you. It is the most powerful of all the chi energies and is therefore treated with respect. If possible, the center of a room or building should be kept clear and open to give this energy room to move.

Tools of the trade

ACETATE
Use to copy the chart of the eight directions on page 41.

COMPASS
Use to orientate the eight directions in your home. Use a standard hiking compass with a flat transparent body, rotating dial, and a clearly marked north-pointing needle.

GRAPH PAPER
Graph paper makes it easier to draw a plan.

MEASURING TAPE
Use to measure up rooms in your home.

PENCILS AND ERASER
Use to produce a clear drawing of your floor plan. Erase mistakes!

MARKER PENS
Use different colors to mark the center and to draw each of the eight directions.

PROTRACTOR
A clear plastic instrument marked with 360 degrees. Use to measure angles.

SCISSORS
Use to cut out the acetate chart.

RULER
Required to draw straight lines on your floor plan and to work out a convenient scale if you are not using graph paper.

FENG SHUI EQUIPMENT

WATER FEATURES
Use to bring more vitality into your home.

SEA SALT
For cleansing the energy at home, and for stabilizing the flow of energy throughout.

WIND CHIMES
The sound of a wind chime sends out ripples of energy, which move and spread out energy. Hang by a door, so each time it is opened the door knocks the tag that hangs down.

CLOCKS
Used for adding rhythm to a space. Choose a clock with a pendulum and as many metal parts as possible.

PLANTS
Use to bring more natural energy into your home. Suitable for all rooms as long as they remain healthy. Plants also help reduce noise and air pollution.

FRESH FLOWERS
Use to bring in more living energy and color to brighten up a room. Brighter colors create a lively atmosphere and pale shades a relaxed feel. Discard as soon as they begin to wilt.

a graph, acetate, and plain
   papers

b compass

c measuring tape

d pencil

e eraser

f protractor

g scissors

h marker pens

i ruler

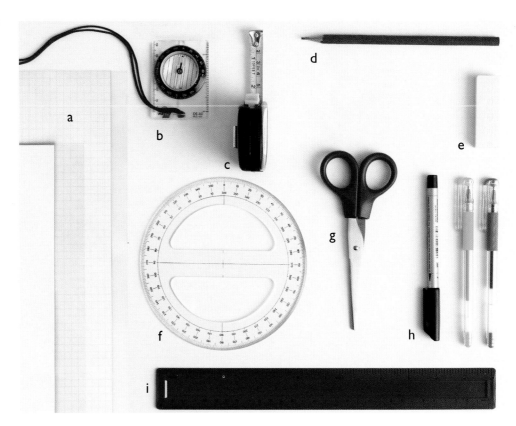

The author with the tools he uses to improve the quality of life for his clients. Of these, the compass is the most important tool, since it gives the basic direction from which all things develop.

CRYSTALS

Use to reflect natural light in all the colors of the rainbow and spread it around the room. Excellent for dark rooms where you want to bring in more natural chi energy.

MIRRORS

Help redirect and keep energy moving. Ideal in rooms that are dark, small or narrow. Ideal for reflecting light.

CONVEX MIRRORS

These round, fish-eye mirrors help disperse chi energy. Use where your stairs lead straight to your front door, or in a long corridor.

CANDLES

Add fiery energy to a space, even though they are more soft than electric lighting. Help to create a passionate and intimate atmosphere.

LIGHTS

Lights add more energy to a room. Uplighters make a room feel taller, indirect lighting is softer, spotlights and halogen lights create an exciting atmosphere, table lamps with shades encourage an intimate feel.

COINS ON A RED CLOTH

This action can help you put more energy into improving your finances.

CHARCOAL

Use artist's charcoal in a clay pot to help harmonize the energy when your have a fireplace, cooker, boiler, or oven in the west or northwest of your home.

Take a compass reading

A compass consists of a body, dial, and needle. The needle is magnetic and will turn to point north. The end of the needle that points north is usually a different color. Check the direction carefully as it is easy to get confused and end up with everything the wrong way around!

The body of the compass is the part you hold in your hand and point toward wherever you want to take a reading. The longer part of the body is the front—this will often also have an arrow marked on it.

The dial is like a wheel around the needle and it is marked with degrees. You turn the dial so that north or zero on the dial lines up with the north tip of the needle. To take a reading, you then look at the degrees on the dial which line up with the line at the front of the body.

The easiest way to take a reading is to stand inside your home and point the compass toward the front wall. You can stand in any room, although it is best to choose a room that has the least electrical equipment and metal items, as they will distort the earth's magnetic field and give a false reading.

To check whether you are getting a true reading, walk around the room holding the compass so it continually points toward the front wall and see if the needle remains steady. If it moves around as you walk, you know the field is distorted and you will have to choose another part of the room, or another room.

Once you have found a stable area, check that the body is pointing exactly to the front wall of the room. Turn the dial and take your reading. Make a note of the reading, since you will need this later.

The easiest way to take a reading is to stand inside your home and point the compass toward the front wall.

Using the sun

If you live in sunny climate, you can get a good feel for the directions by knowing where the sun enters your home at different times of the day. The morning sun will come into your home from the east, the midday sun from the south (or north if you live in the southern hemisphere), and the sunset from the west.

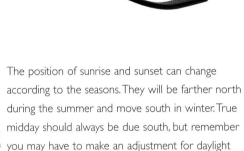

Locate your home on a street map and note which direction it faces. A home on a street pointing to the top of the map faces approximately north.

The position of sunrise and sunset can change according to the seasons. They will be farther north during the summer and move south in winter. True midday should always be due south, but remember you may have to make an adjustment for daylight saving in the summer.

If you want to be more accurate, you can stick a long, wooden skewer or toothpick into a piece of cardboard. Place the cardboard so it lines up with the front of your home on a plan, and mark off the shadow at say 6 a.m., 12 p.m., and 6 p.m. Remove the skewer or toothpick and draw lines from the hole through each of your marks. This should give you east, south, and west respectively.

Originally, a feng shui consultant would have studied a site for several days, and one of the observations taken would have been the way the sun fell onto the dwellings on the site. They would have used a tall, wooden pole to take their reading. If you want to develop these skills, you will be going back to the roots of feng shui. The only practical problem is if you live in a city where the sun doesn't shine every day—this observation won't work!

If all else fails, look at a street map to see which way north is. North will usually be at the top of the page. In some cities, like New York, most of the streets run east to west and north to south, making your work much easier.

Draw a floor plan

This seems like a challenge but, trust me—if you take it one step at a time, it is a lot easier than you think. Basically, you are going to put a series of boxes (rectangles) representing each room next to each other on a piece of paper. To decide how big to make each box you will need to begin by measuring each room.

Use a tape measure and make a note of the length and width of each room. As the exact scale is not important you can equally pace out each room and make a note of how many paces it takes to walk from one end to the other.

Next, you need to think of a convenient scale. For example, you could say 3 feet (approx. 1 meter) equals half an inch (1.3cm), or one foot (approx. 30.5cm) equals one-sixteenth of an inch (2mm).

Step one: start with a room in one corner of your home. Using your scale, draw a box on a sheet of paper representing the size of the room. You may find it easier to use squared graph paper so you can simply count off the squares.

Step two: move onto another room and draw another rectangle next to your first. Continue in this way until you have all the rooms in the home in the correct place. If your home has more than one floor you will need to do the same thing for each floor, using a separate sheet of paper.

Step three: sketch in all the items that will help you work out where everything is in your home. This would normally include windows, doors, stairs, toilets, sinks, baths, showers, dishwasher, washing machine, stove, boiler, and fireplaces.

Use sticky notes to cut out shapes to represent your furniture, since they will be easy to move around the graph sheet.

If you are computer literate, you can do the same thing in Microsoft Word™ or PowerPoint™. Simply draw rectangles and put in the dimensions by clicking on size on the formatting bar.

Use a ruler or something with a straight edge to draw lines. Start at one corner of the paper with one corner of your home, so the plan will fit on the page. Draw lines firmly and as straight as you can if you don't have a ruler!

Find the center

The simplest shape of which to find the center is a rectangle. If your home is rectangular, or close to a rectangle, you can draw a diagonal line between the corners, and the point at which they cross will be the center. You can ignore small extensions, such as a porch or little indentation, and just draw a rectangle.

Draw the main walls of your rooms firmly with a thick line. Use thin dotted lines for finding the center, so your drawing remains clear.

If you live in an apartment, you need only include the areas that are for your sole use and not any corridors or halls that are shared with people from other apartments.

Where your home has an "L" shape, it is more complicated. To find the center, you need to divide your home into two rectangles. Draw diagonal lines across each rectangle to find the centers using a light-colored pencil and then draw a line between the two centers. We know the center of the entire shape will be somewhere along this line.

Now divide the shape into two different rectangles, using a different color, but use the two different rectangles. Again, draw diagonal lines to find the centers and then draw a line between these new centers. This line will cross the line you previously drew between the original centers and this point marks the center of the entire shape.

If you have a more complicated shape, you can draw it onto a piece of stiff cardboard and cut it out to the same shape as your home.

Push a pin through the cardboard close to one of the corners. Make sure the cardboard can swivel freely on the pin. Hold the cardboard up by the pin and put the pin next to a vertical edge. It is best to use a triangular square, although a book will do. Mark a line on the piece of cardboard running straight down from the pin. Do the same again with the pin pushed through the board close to another corner. Where the two lines cross will be the center.

Lay on the eight directions

The easiest way to lay the eight directions over your floor plan is to photocopy the facing page (page 41) onto an acetate. This is the kind of transparency used in overhead projectors and available at most copy centers.

A FINAL PLAN

The drawing above was created on my computer in Microsoft PowerPoint™ (you can also use Word™). The color blocks represent the directions. Important details are printed on each color for easy reference. The information is the same as on the transparency wheel opposite, just laid out in a different way. If you have a computer, you can easily draw a plan like the one above and use it as a template for other plans, inventing symbols for recommendations, and a key as a guide. Put the information on each color box and move each color box to its relevant direction position on the drawing. When you draw up plans for friends, they can see the directions and the recommendations at a glance.

1. Take the acetate sheet and cut around the outer perimeter of the diagram so you have a circle with all the information on it.

2. Next: on your floor plan, draw a line, using a new color, from the center of your home straight through the front of your home.

3. Put the eight directions transparency over the floor plan so the center of the transparency is over the center of the floor plan. You may find it easier to stick a pin through the transparency and floor plan to keep them in place.

4. Now turn the transparency so the compass reading you took when facing the front of your home (page 36) is the same as the reading on the transparency where it meets the line from the center to the front of your home.

You have now correctly aligned the eight directions and can have a look at where each direction is in your home. Your transparency tells you the direction, trigram, and five element, so you know what kind of energy is present in that part of your home. Also included are suggestions for colors and materials for flooring, furniture, and surfaces in that part of your home.

Finally, I have added some notes on what that part of your home is good for and a suggestion for boosting the energy there.

You can mark the ends of the eight directions onto your floor plan and then draw the eight directions onto your plan using another color if you want a permanent record.

In this system the four cardinal points—north, south, east, and west—represent fixed points—midnight, sunrise, midday, and sunset. These each have 30 degrees, and the remaining changing directions have 60 degrees.

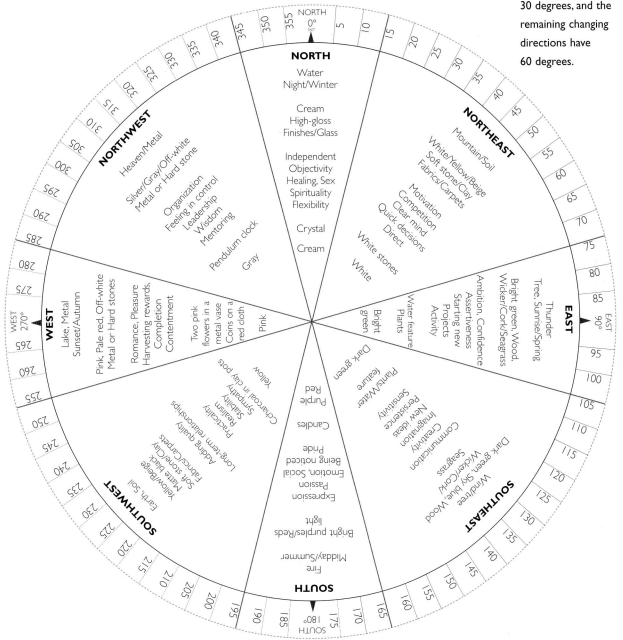

This section is dedicated to showing you specific actions you can take, using feng shui principles, to make your life instantaneously better! Try a few of them, once you have worked out the problems, and see what happens next.

Instant

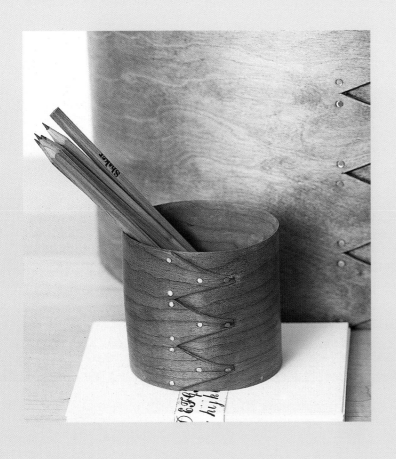

Feng shui

For a good night's sleep

In my experience in both using feng shui and advising others, the direction in which you sleep has the greatest influence on your life. The good news is that this powerful feng shui life enhancer is free—it costs nothing to turn your bed around!

It is easy to experiment with different sleeping directions. Simply turn your bed and try it out for six to twelve weeks and make a note of any changes you might experience.

When you go to sleep your chi energy becomes more passive and receptive as it recharges itself. Your body is busy regenerating and repairing cells. At this time you take in more energy, and it is important to ensure you take in the kind of chi energy that will be helpful to you. As most chi energy will enter your body through the crown chakra, where the spiral is on the top of your head, which way the top of your head points is important.

When you wake up, you will contain more of the energy absorbed through the crown chakra and this can color your day. To make this work for you, first decide what will help you be successful in life. Then look at the following pages to decide which energy would be most helpful to you.

It is also possible that you may be sleeping with the top of your head pointing in a direction that could be holding you back. For example, if you feel over-emotional, stressed, and don't sleep well, sleeping with the top of your head pointing south will make things worse. South is a fiery, active, potentially explosive chi energy.

The bedroom layout may limit the directions you can face. Doors, windows, and fitted storage can work against you. Turn the bed to the best direction, anyway, to see how it feels. Notice an improvement? Explore ways to make it permanent. Otherwise, find another direction that's close to serving your needs.

When setting up a bedroom, keep its arrangement flexible so you can move the bed to different positions when necessary. You will go through different phases in life, and could benefit from a change of chi energy. Use freestanding storage units rather than built-in ones.

Once you know which energy you would like more of, check which direction it is associated with. To find the current direction, hold the compass over the bed so the body is pointing up to your pillow. Turn the dial so 0 degrees lines up with the north tip of the needle. Make a note of the reading, and look at the eight directions transparency to see which direction that reading relates to.

You can also lay the transparency on the bed and turn it so the correct reading is pointing up to your pillows. You can easily see which way to turn the bed to get the energy you want.

Do the same thing on your floor plan. Draw a line from the center of your bedroom to the front of your home. Place the center of the transparency over the center of the room and turn it until the correct reading is over the line. Work out how to turn the bed to get the direction you want.

In addition to the direction, keep the energy of your bedroom more yin and quiet. Use softer materials and make sure there are no sharp edges pointing at the bed. Keep all doors and window coverings closed at night to help contain the chi energy and reduce the risk of it flowing through your bedroom too quickly. Mirrors and shiny objects can make the chi energy buzz around your room and interfere with your sleep. It helps if the mirrors do not point at your bed.

Here, Simon's head and chakra (when laid on the pillow) will face east. Sleeping with your head facing east is good for younger people. This energy makes you wake up eager to get on with the day, and is useful if you have to get up early.

Head in the right direction!

This spread helps you decide in which direction to have the top of your head pointing. Read through the advantages of the direction in which you are currently sleeping, then read through the rest to see if there is another direction that better suits your needs.

SOUTHWEST

This is a good direction to sleep to feel more settled. The sun is moving down in the afternoon sky. The benefits are helpful for finding ways to improve the quality of your life. This can result in better relationships, a happier family life, and greater satisfaction at work. It is also helpful for good sleep, particularly if you have trouble settling down at night. Also use it to be homey, practical, and realistic.

SOUTH

This hot, fiery energy makes this direction help you feel more passionate, expressive, and social. It is not good for anyone who has trouble sleeping, gets stressed easily, or is argumentative. It can be a mentally stimulating energy and it can help sharpen your mind. I would not recommend it to anyone who is having arguments in their relationship, but it is ideal if you are single and want to get noticed.

SOUTHEAST

This energy is associated with the sun moving up in the sky and spring changing to summer, making it helpful for generally feeling up and eager to get on with your life. It is excellent for communication, relationships, imagination, and increased creativity. I find it to be an energy that helps with new ideas. It can also help you be persistent and work toward your long-term goals.

EAST

Eastern energy is ideal for younger people. This "beginning of the day's springtime energy" helps you to wake up feeling eager to get on with the day. It is useful if you have difficulty getting up early. Over time, sleeping in this direction is helpful for being more ambitious, getting things done, and being more active. It is excellent for building up your life and starting new projects.

WEST

Western chi energy combines the benefits of good sleep with feelings of contentment. This romantic, sunset energy is ideal for relationships and a good sleeping direction if you want to have more fun in bed. It can help you be more playful and youthful. As is relates to the harvest time, it helps you with your finances, and completing things.

NORTHWEST

Sleeping with your head pointing northwest is helpful in terms of getting more evening end-of-the-year energy. It can help you get a long, deep, sleep. It also brings more energy associated with leadership, responsibility, and feeling in control of things. This mature energy could be too serious if you are young and may be better suited to someone who is already established in life.

NORTH

Turning the bed so the top of your head points north is ideal for anyone who has sleeping problems. North is a very quiet direction, which makes it ideal for you if you need to calm down in general. This direction will enhance feelings of peace and tranquility, and bring you closer to the spiritual world. It can also help you feel more intimate, affectionate, and sexual, however, it is usually too quiet for a young person.

NORTHEAST

This energy can be too hard and piercing for good sleep and could have the effect of making you feel on edge. It may even increase the risk of nightmares. The advantage is that it helps you feel more motivated, decisive, and competitive. It can be useful if you want to get a clearer sense of direction in life. I rarely recommend this direction for sleeping except if someone wants a drastic change in life.

Kick your shoes off!

Everyone wants to relax. We need moments to escape and unwind so we can come back refreshed. The way you arrange the seating will determine the kind of energy you absorb into your own energy field and will have a bearing on how you feel.

When arranging seating, remember to protect your back with a wall, a large piece of furniture, or a large plant, and keep the area in front of you open.

First, to check the direction you already face when seated in your chair, hold the compass with the body pointing away from you, turn the dial so that 0 degrees is lined up with the north end of the needle, then take a reading from where the dial lines up with the center of the body.

Note the reading and then look at the chart on page 41 to see which direction it relates to. For example, 23 degrees will be northeast. Find the direction on the opposite page and see how it can influence you.

Read through the other directions to find out if there is another energy that may help you more. For example, if you find it hard to settle down facing the more piercing northeastern energy, facing settled southwestern energy would make it easier.

N

Face north when you want to forget the stresses of the day, and you will recover your sanity. Most of all, make yourself comfortable.

EAST

This is a good direction to face if you want to feel more positive and confident. It is not very relaxing, as you may find you are thinking about what to do next, but good if you need to boost your self-esteem. It is also a good position if you want to concentrate on something, such as reading a book.

SOUTHEAST

Facing southeast is great if you want to daydream and let your imagination run wild. Although still an up energy (the sun is moving up the morning sky), it is more gentle and relaxing than facing east. This direction is helpful when you want to think about the future and run through all your options.

SOUTH

The fiery midday southern energy is excellent for feeling more expressive and outgoing. This is the best direction in which to sit if you want to feel more social. It is helpful when you have friends round or you want to entertain. When you are alone, it is not particularly relaxing and could make you feel more sensitive to stress.

SOUTHWEST

This settled afternoon energy is useful to take in when you need to get your feet back on the ground and feel more secure. It can help bring your energy down if you are feeling that your head is too busy. Southwest is associated with harmonious long-term relationships, so it is a helpful direction to feel closer to your loved ones.

WEST

Sitting facing the autumn (sunset energy of the west), helps makes your energy more inward. This helps you feel more content and at ease with yourself. West is also good when you want to feel more romantic and this would be the ideal direction to face when you are on a date. Avoid this direction when you feel withdrawn or low.

NE

Northeast is a helpful direction to face when playing games. It might help you find a winning streak.

NORTHWEST

Northwestern energy is associated with the evening and the end of the year, so it would be a helpful direction to face when you want to review your life and consider what you have learned so far. It is ideal for feeling relaxed and letting your intuition and natural wisdom take over. It is not helpful if you tend to be too serious, or if you are a control freak.

NORTH

This is the ideal direction for rest and relaxation. The stillness of the night and winter associated with this energy helps you calm down and go with the flow. It is a direction that is well suited to finding that inner peace and one that I recommend for meditation or any kind of spiritual practice.

NORTHEAST

Sitting facing northeast is helpful when you need greater mental clarity, or you have to make a decision you have been putting off. It is a helpful energy for card or board games. As it can be sharp and piercing, I would not recommend it purely for relaxing.

Work directions

Working from home is a pleasure. Apart from not having to commute, you have total control over your environment and can create a space that really works for you. You can sit facing a variety of directions to enjoy the benefits of different influences.

Not only can you create the best environment but you can also have the music you like, access to fresh air and natural light. This is much healthier than being stuck in an office with artificial lighting and air conditioning. People can find it more stressful working in environments over which they feel they have no control.

If you have the opportunity to work from home look through the directions below and see which ones will help you most. You may find one direction is better for certain aspects of your work, and another for a different task. Experiment to see what works best. If you work in an office, you may still be able to alter the direction you face even if it means turning your desk slightly. Use the compass method (see page 48) to find out which direction you are currently facing, and then decide which direction you need to face and change it.

SE

Take the time to arrange your work area and your desk because, when everything faces the right direction, you will work happily and more successfully.

EAST

This is a good direction to face if you want to make your ideas a reality. It is excellent for concentration and being focused on one thing. You feel more ambitious sitting facing this direction, and more eager to get on with everything. The morning, springtime eastern energy is ideal for starting new projects or starting a new career.

SOUTHEAST

Facing southeast is excellent if you want to get new ideas and your work requires you to use your imagination. As this direction is associated with wind, it is useful if your work requires you to communicate and spread your ideas. Try this direction if you need to be creative. It is also generally helpful for moving forward in your career and working through challenges.

SOUTH

The fiery midday southern energy is perfect for getting noticed. Use this energy to develop your reputation and get your name known. It is an energy that helps you feel mentally stimulated, and slightly in front of everyone else. Try this direction when you need to promote yourself or make sales calls. This energy would not be helpful if you are trying to concentrate or focus on something for long periods.

SOUTHWEST

This settled afternoon energy is useful for being practical and working methodically through something. It helps you be realistic and careful. The essence of this energy is to take what you have and make it better so it is ideal when you want to improve the quality of what you are doing. I would also recommend it for developing long-term relationships with your clients.

WEST

Sitting facing end-of-the-day sunset energy from the west helps you complete things and focus on the end result. As this energy relates to the harvest time it is helpful for bringing in the rewards of your hard work. This means finding ways to increase your profits and get more investment. You can use this energy for greater financial awareness, but be careful, as it can also encourage overspending.

NORTHWEST

Northwestern energy is associated with the heavens and your father so it is associated with having a mentor and leadership. This energy is helpful for feeling more organized and in control of things. It is particularly useful for long-term planning and getting a clearer idea of where you are going. Also use it to help yourself be perceived as someone who is trustworthy, has integrity, and is responsible.

NORTH

This watery nighttime energy is helpful for being flexible and going with the flow. It is also associated with being independent and objective. I find it very useful when you want to step outside of yourself and what you are doing and get a fresh look. Northern energy is ideal for thinking up original ideas and can help when you want to just work calmly by yourself.

NORTHEAST

Working facing northeast is helpful when you need to be more competitive and put more energy into winning things. This sharp, piercing energy can help you be more ruthless and quick to seize new opportunities. Try it when you need to be more clear minded, decisive, and focused on your goals. It is useful for being motivated and energetic about getting to where you want to be.

Clearing clutter

The quickest and most dramatic way to change your energy and the energy of your home is to do a complete spring cleaning. You will feel like a new person, and it is also great way to lift your mood.

One of the aims of feng shui is to encourage chi energy to move harmoniously through your home. This makes it easier to lead a well-balanced life and get the best of everything. It is important to avoid situations where the chi energy stagnates, as this will make it harder for you to do things with your life, and could make it harder to maintain good health.

One of the things that makes chi energy stagnate is clutter. Too much clutter restricts the movement of chi energy and encourages it to lose its momentum. Living in this environment could make you feel lazy, unmotivated, and uninspired. It could even make you more prone to feeling depressed or feeling that you can't be bothered to make an effort.

You can usually tell where chi energy has stagnated as this will also be where dust has collected. The quickest way to change this is to have a major spring clean. By taking everything out of its place and cleaning all those dark corners you will stir up all the chi energy that has lain dormant.

Once you have got everything out of its place you need to attack the empty spaces with your cleaning materials and get every bit of dirt and dust out of your home. It is best to do this on a dry sunny day. Keep the windows open so lots of fresh chi energy will blow through your home.

If you have a garden take as much clutter out into the sun as you can so it can be exposed to the natural elements. Particularly important are any textiles such as curtains, rugs, and cushions. Take them out and beat all the dust out of them. This can be therapeutic in itself if you have some frustrations to be rid of! Think of someone who has annoyed you recently while you do it!

Once you have gotten everything out of your home, shampoo any carpets, as this is where most of the dust and stagnant energy tends to collect. It is even worth washing painted walls if you feel up to it.

Also, thoroughly clean all areas where you keep or prepare food. This includes shelves, fridge, stove, and in particula,r behind appliances. It is vital that the chi energy surrounding the food you are going to eat is healthy as it will affect the chi energy in the food and you will eventually eat this food!

Now is the most convenient time to think about getting rid of clutter. Before you put everything back, start to look at what you really need. You may find there is lots of stuff you no longer need that is just getting in the way of everyday routines.

People who travel a lot, or move from country to country or city to city in their career, taking the family with them, are used to clearing out the clutter of their existence. Traveling light is the norm! You could learn from this edit-as-you-go existence, and be rid of some of your accumulated material possessions to benefit your future. All it takes is the courage to acknowledge people do not need many possessions to be happy.

Chi energy will move more easily across clear surfaces. Be careful not to make your home too sterile or lifeless by taking this concept of clutter clearing too far!

For some people the only way to clear clutter is to sit on the floor with the clutter spread around them. That way they can sift through and throw away what's not needed. Choose a day to clear clutter and make it fun! Try not to become tense or you may contaminate the energy.

STORAGE

It is important to make your storage as functional as possible. Everything needs to be accessible, out of the way, easy to clean, and to look good. You need to match all the stuff you want to store with the space you have available.

Put all the items you need to store in the middle of the room and sort them out into how you want to store them, how often you need them and where they should be. For example, divide into hanging, shelving, or boxes. Some things will need to be relocated to the bedroom, bathroom, or kitchen.

For long-term storage you can use your loft or garage. Even though these place are often out of sight it is important to invest in proper storage systems so you can find everything when you need it.

BOX IT!

The biggest challenge in getting rid of clutter is deciding what you really need and what is just getting in the way. Also, some clutter may have strong associations with the past and be holding you back. It could be a relief to let go of it and move forward again.

Clutter can hang onto energy, and keep chi energy in a place for longer periods of time. This can lead to a stuffy feeling, where it is harder to feel active and able to do more in life. In extreme cases, the person living in a very cluttered home can feel that everything is a struggle and that they are stuck in a rut. When you want to move forward, and let go of the past, get rid of clutter, and open up your home so that it is easier for the chi energy to flow. This will make it easier for you to make a fresh start.

Another aspect to think about is that during your life you may have experienced difficult times. Although you now want to move on, it would be more difficult if you keep the energy of these old experiences in your home in the form of the clutter that went with it. For example, if you had a bad ending to a relationship and you were finding it difficult to let go and start a new relationship, it would make it worse to keep reminders of that relationship in your home.

To make it easier to decide what you can get rid of, and what you should keep, get a number of large cardboard boxes and label each one with today's

Open storage units make it easy to display things you love and make it easy to find something when you need it! The disadvantage is that the shelves will need to be dusted regularly. Do not put too many things in this type of unit as it could easily become a site for new clutter.

Choose natural materials for units to store items such as facecloths and guest soaps. Making the arrangement both attractive and tidy adds to a sense of order. A natural woven basket such as this is ideal as a bathroom accessory.

Many storage items are sold ready to assemble. You don't need a degree in carpentry, just a screwdriver and a strong wrist. And the ability to read the instructions! Free-standing units are best since you can take them with you when you move.

SHAKER STYLE

Natural products are best in any home or office environment. Here, a traditional shaker box has been adapted to file business or household accounts. It is beautiful to look at, and practical.

date. Clearly label them "long-term storage," "letting go," and "undecided."

Put all the things that you think you will not need for some time in the "long-term storage" box. This could include financial information you are obliged to keep for a number of years, things that have sentimental value such old letters, photos, gifts you were given and dislike, and reminders of ancestors, as well as things that could be important to your children (if you have children).

Next, take the box marked "letting go" and put in it all the items that remind you of a part of your life's history that you wish to leave behind. This could include items such as photographs, nonessential documents, and letters.

Now take the "undecided" box and put into it all the things that clutter your home, but you are not sure you will miss. For instance, personal papers, clothing, household items, decorative objects, and artwork.

Wait a month and then throw out everything in the "letting go" box if you have not missed them. Keep the other two boxes for another month and look through them to see if you can transfer anything from "undecided" to "long-term storage," or from "long-term storage" to "undecided." Repeat every month, and see after three months if you feel comfortable parting with the contents of the "undecided" box.

Do this every year to stop new clutter from building up. Better yet, stop yourself buying things that will soon become clutter. You may find it easier to have a few high quality items that will last a lifetime rather than lots of things that will either break or become obsolete in a few years.

Labeling boxes is
an important step in
the path to clarity
in both your business and
personal lives. It also
saves time when you're
looking for something!

Corner cover-ups

Any corner that points into a room will direct fast-flowing energy into your living space. This can be a problem if it funnels the energy toward a place where you like to sleep or relax. The result is that you would feel unsettled, on edge, and tense. It can result in poor sleep and increase the risk of poor health in the long term.

It is important to check all the places you and other people living with you sleep and relax to see if there are any corners pointing at you. Tall corners or long edges, such as a sharp beam, are of most concern as they direct a significant amount of energy, whereas the corner of a table will not have as much effect.

The aim is to make the corners softer or, when possible, rounder. The easiest way to do this is to put a plant in front of the corner. The plant will soften up the edge and protect you from any fast-flowing energy. In addition the plant has its own living chi energy field, which will make it harder for the fast flowing chi energy from the corner to pass through.

CORNER ENERGY

1
Take three lengths of ribbon, each a different width and texture, and attach them to the top of the corner. Neatly trim the edges.

2
Tie a trim such as this attractive beaded one, on the end of one of the ribbons.

3
Tie a neat bow as a finishing touch. The trim keeps one ribbon anchored in place, and the breeze can catch the others and distract the energy.

The plant should be at least head height so that your full body is protected. Use a yin, bushy plant with dense foliage so that it will be effective in slowing the energy. In situations where you cannot have a plant standing on the floor, use a hanging plant. Hang the plant container from the ceiling just in front of the corner and let the plant trail down in front of the corner.

When you cannot use a plant, hang a fabric ribbon (see steps on these pages), or drape a piece of soft fabric in front of the corner to soften it. Alternatively, look for a decorative screen to place in front of the sharp edge.

ROUND IT OFF

If you are having a new home built or are renovating your home, round off the protruding corners wherever possible to avoid the problem altogether. You only need to get a similar radius to a coffee mug and it will make your whole home feel softer and more harmonious.

Your home could be subjected to fast flowing chi energy if the corner of another building is pointing toward you. This could make your home feel less relaxing. The remedy is to plant bushes and trees between the corner and your home. In addition, you could put something convex and reflective on the outside of your home pointing back at the corner. This could be a small convex mirror or a shiny metal plate. The reflective surface will direct some of the fast-flowing energy back and away from your home.

For this protruding corner, a length of crystal beading was attached to the top of the corner to hang down over the offending edge. Any breeze wafting past swings it gently.

Inside story

The corners in your room are prime areas where energy can

stagnate. Here, the energy gets stuck in corners and makes the

atmosphere feel heavy. It can make your life feel as if it

is dragging, and not as exciting as it could be.

A hanging plant is sometimes more convenient than a free-standing plant. This plant will speed up the energy as it passes by and prevent the energy becoming too yin.

It is more likely that energy will get stuck when you have a lot of things in corners. Shelves, chairs, or display cabinets can all clutter up corners. The challenge is to find ways to keep the chi energy moving through your corners. Try to keep the corners of your rooms as open as possible, so they are easy to get into, and the chi energy there remains fresh.

The answer is to use objects that radiate chi energy of their own. Examples of this would be plants, lights, or something that produces sound. In terms of plants it would be best to use yang ones with pointed leaves as these are better at stirring up energy and getting it moving.

I often recommend putting an uplighter into a corner. This will add more yang dynamic energy into the corner in the evening when it is lit. Position the light behind a plant to create a dramatic lighting effect.

Sound waves will stir up the air in a corner so it is good to have a stereo speaker in the corner. In our home, we have a light, a yucca plant, and a telephone in the corner of the living room, which combine to keep the energy flowing easily through that corner.

Keep the corners tidy and clean, as it is much easier for dust to build up in corners. Also, corners are a convenient place to put things you have no proper place for. Stop doing that!

If you feel the energy in a corner is stagnant, ring a hand bell there, or clap your hands loudly to help activate the energy more. It works, believe me.

A potted pointed leaf plant placed in a corner will stimulate the energy and make the area more yang, reducing the risk of stagnation.

Cleansing rituals

At times, your home can take on a negative atmosphere. This could be the result of a bitter argument, or because you are just feeling depressed. The emotions radiated during these times will fill your home so it could have an angry or depressive feeling.

Try to move on from these feelings and change the atmosphere in your home because it is important these feelings do not stay in your home and return to you. Using sea salt is one way to help this process. The salt is very yang and in a similar way that salt absorbs dampness from the atmosphere, it also absorbs chi energy.

Use salt to soak up the negative energy, allowing fresh, new energy to come into your home to replace it. Sprinkle sea salt on the floors of the rooms that you feel are a problem before going to bed. In the morning, vacuum or sweep up the salt. Remember to remove salt from your home immediately, so you get rid of the negative chi energy.

You can repeat this exercise several times until you feel your home has a fresh, clean atmosphere and you find it easier to move on. This process will be more powerful if you combine it with spring cleaning and clearing clutter (see pages 52 to 55). For example, if you have come to the end of a relationship, apart from the usual custom of throwing all of his or her clothes out the window, it will help you to move on and let go of that relationship if you give your home a major spring cleaning, get rid of as much clutter as possible, especially things that relate to the relationship, and sprinkle sea salt throughout your home at night.

It is also good feng shui practice to keep a bowl of sea salt in the northeast and southwest parts of your home.

1
Pour two tablespoons of fresh sea salt into a natural ceramic container. Or just guess!

2
Place the container with the sea salt in the northeast part of your home. Repeat in the southwest part.

The energy in these directions is less stable and placing sea salt in these two places helps make your home feel more stable.

Lay the transparency over the floor plan and check which parts of your home are to the northeast and the southwest. Locate a suitable place in which to put the sea salt.

I recommend putting two tablespoons in a small ramekin dish, as its flat bottom makes it secure. This is particularly helpful if you have any external doors or large windows in these directions.

Preferably, put the sea salt on the floor, or place the container inside a cupboard, or behind a door if that is more convenient. If you have children or pets you will need to keep it out of reach. Change the sea salt every two months.

NE

Changing the energy

You can change the atmosphere of your home with your own energy. Your thoughts and emotions will radiate from your body and mix with the chi energy of your home. Simply playing dance music and jumping around your home will pick up and refresh the atmosphere making the space feel more yang.

To surround yourself with the kind of energy that helps you live the way you want to live, you need to put more of that energy into your home.

One way to do this would be to meditate and focus your mind strongly on what you are trying to achieve. Each time you breathe out, imagine you are breathing those thoughts out into the room.

The sound of a bell will help send your own chi energy out further. As you ring the bell, the sound waves ripple through your home carrying your chi energy with it. Keep a hand bell with you and ring it when you have a thought or feeling you want to send out strongly.

Hand bells are also useful for stirring up stagnant energy. If your home feels flat, take a hand bell and ring it in all the corners and anywhere that dust usually collects. The sound waves will help get the energy moving again and encourage fresh chi energy into those areas.

Just as it will improve the energy of your home to project positive feelings into it, it can also affect the energy if you fill your home with negative emotions. If you are feeling low, it would help to go out for a walk and take in different energy while keeping your emotions out of your home for a while. When you return, it will have a more uplifting feeling. Similarly, if you need to have a talk with someone that may become heated, arrange to have the discussion out of your home.

N

Meditation is a wonderfully relaxing and cleansing ritual. Find a comfortable place to sit, with your spine straight. Breathe deeply into your abdomen. Think positive thoughts and exhale them into the room.

Dancing or jumping around will stir up your chi energy and make it easier to project your energy into a room. This helps you feel more yang. Star jumps are fun, too!

Ring-a-ding-a-ling! Ringing a hand bell will send ripples of energy, carried by sound waves, through your energy field and out into the room.

Symbolism to go!

Have you noticed that people who live alone, and want to be in a relationship, display lots of images of single people, and arrange the objects in their home in a space of their own? Here, we'll look at how the imagery in your home will influence you by triggering certain thought patterns.

It is helpful to ensure the imagery in your home is in keeping with what you want to achieve in life. Anything, such photographs, paintings, and objects, has an influence. Walk around your home and take a careful look at everything to see if it is really encouraging you. Anything that reminds you of something you are moving away from should be moved into storage. Then, see how you feel without it after a few months.

If being in a relationship is important to you, keeping things in pairs can send out the right message to your unconscious mind. For example, putting two plants in the same pot would symbolize two living things sharing the same home. Similarly, keep a picture of people

1

Take a ceramic plant container and fill it with fresh potting soil. If the container does not have a hole in the bottom, add a layer of stones in the bottom for good drainage.

2

Take one of the similar plants and gently replant it in the larger container. Add the second plant, pushing in the soil firmly.

close together, sculptures of couples in an embrace, and arrange romantic objects, such as candles, in pairs around the home.

Put pictures of anything that inspires you so you can see them. If you really want to buy your own home, keep a picture of your dream palace on the wall. This will help drive you forward to achieve your aim.

Think clearly about what you want in life, and then find images that are as close as possible to your desires. Equally, it is important to display imagery that reminds you of your past successes. Photographs of happy times, awards, or examples of work you are proud of are all good for maintaining self-esteem.

3

Firmly press the soil to bed them securely and lightly water the soil. Yellow plants are helpful when placed in the southwest or west part of your home.

In the following pages, we look at an important area: relationships. We look at six aspects, offering easy-to-follow solutions that get results, and can help to make your relationship a success.

Fix-its

Relationships

Lover, where art thou?

Generally speaking, in my experience, men and women of all ages and experiences and of all socioeconomic groups, want to find a lover at some time in their lives.

If you have not been successful in starting a new relationship, begin by thinking how you can improve your chances. Do you need to meet more people, be better at initiating a relationship, or have greater confidence in yourself? Choose one specific topic or, if you are feeling enthusiastic, do them all.

1

Take a photo frame with an image of you on your own. Find a photo of you with someone important in your life.

WANT TO FEEL ROMANTIC?

West will help you feel more romantic, playful, and fun-loving. This direction could help you attract a new lover. To absorb more of this energy, sleep with the top of your head pointing west. Hold a compass over your bed to see which way you would have to turn it to sleep with your head facing that direction.

Use your floor plan and transparency, or watch the position of the setting sun, to find the west part of your bedroom or the west part of your entire home.

Find a suitable place in this direction to put a vase with two flowers. The area should be clean and free from clutter. Put two pink or red flowers into a silver-colored metal vase, and place in the area you have prepared. Hang a small round or oval mirror behind the flowers to increase their influence. Refill the vase every day with fresh water and cut a little piece off the end of the stems to keep the flowers fresh. Discard as soon as they begin to wilt.

2

Replace the single image with the one of you together.

WANT TO BE MORE SOCIAL AND EXPRESSIVE?

South is ideal for being more social, outgoing, passionate, and expressive. If you need to meet more people, that's the way you've got to be. Try sleeping with the top of your head pointing south to absorb more fiery, southern energy.

Find the south part of your bedroom or whole home and prepare a space so that there is nothing combustible nearby. Place two candles close together on a bright purple cloth. Hang a star-shaped or triangular mirror behind the candles to increase the effect. Light the candles every day. This will focus your energy on sociability.

WANT MORE CONFIDENCE?

Southeast is a good direction to try when you want to feel more confident about starting a relationship. This morning energy can help you feel inspired and better able to come up with new ideas for finding a new lover. Sleeping with the top of your head pointing southeast will help you absorb more southeastern energy.

Locate the southeastern part of your home, and place a bowl of water in the area. Empty and refill the bowl with fresh water every day as soon as you get up.

PREPARE FOR A RELATIONSHIP

Imagine you are already in a relationship, and make sure your home would be comfortable for two people. For example, sleep in a large bed, sit on a sofa, and eat at a table designed for two. This will help you feel ready for accepting someone into your life, and help you feel more comfortable about the process of being in a relationship.

3

Place it in the west part of your home.

Take care of what you have

The energy of the southwest is great for making the most of an existing relationship. This energy relates to summer changing to fall, and fruit ripening on the vine. It is all about taking something you have and making it better. It's also good for feeling more caring, and enjoying being part of a family unit.

Bringing more southwestern energy into your home will help you put more energy into your relationship and find ways to make it better. You can bring more of this energy into your own chi energy field by turning your bed so you each sleep with the top of your head pointing southwest.

Find the southwest part of your home using your floor plan and transparency, or by looking at the direction the sun descends in the afternoon sky. To activate the southwestern energy in your home place fresh yellow flowers, or a yellow flowering plant, in a earthenware container in this part of your home. You could also use more yellows in your home.

Fresh yellow flowers in a decorative terra cotta pot bring more settled soil energy into the southwest part of your home helping to stabilize a relationship.

Using the principles of the five elements you can support the southwestern earth chi energy with fire. Do it by placing a pair of candles in the southwest part of your home. Light them daily for a while to get the fire energy into this part of your home.

Try sitting together facing southwest and discuss ways in which you both can improve your relationship. In these moments it is essential you each make positive suggestions on how you can contribute more rather than one person tell the other what he or she should do. Avoid criticizing each other as you will quickly start to go backward. Try to listen to each other and really hear what the other person is saying without jumping in with your own comments.

If you have an object representing fire energy in the west of your home, harmonize these possibly destructive fire chi energies with more soil energy in the form of charcoal. Fire energy can destroy the romance of the west.

Move closer

When you are in a long-term relationship, the partnership takes on an energy of its own. This energy is a mixture of both of your chi energies. The more time you spend together, the more your energies mix. If you sleep together your chi energy fields will merge, and you will feel closer to your lover. In theory, you will unconsciously pick up each other's thoughts and emotions in the process.

Wear a lover's shirt or perhaps their watch when you want to bring some of their energy into your own energy field.

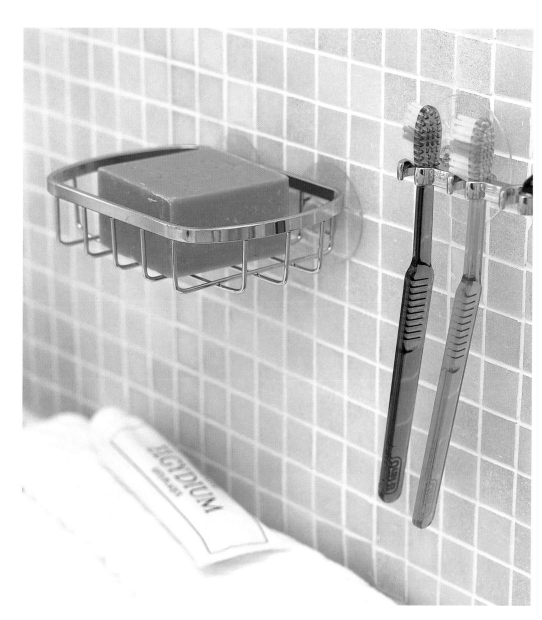

Keeping your personal things together mixes some of your chi energy that has attached itself to the items. This helps reinforce the feeling of togetherness.

One way you can feel closer is to take something that has your lover's energy and keep this within your chi energy field. This would have to be something your lover usually keeps within his or her energy field, such as clothing, nightclothes, a bracelet, a necklace, or a watch.

Wearing his or her personal items will bring some of your lover's energy into your chi energy field, making it easier to feel closer and more intimate. This can be reassuring if you have to be apart for some time. Traditionally, people would take a lock of their lover's hair in a silver locket when they went away on a long journey.

You can also encourage this process by using symbolism. For example, keeping your toothbrushes, hairbrushes, and shoes close together or even mixing

some of your clothes when hanging them in a closet, or storing them, will reinforce the feeling of togetherness, and reinforce the reality of you sharing each other's lives.

Similarly it is always helpful to keep photographs of you both having fun together in a prominent place and look at them frequently to remind yourself of the good times.

Choose romance

One way to be romantic is to share a meal with the one you love.
As food and sex both relate to our primal instincts for survival,
the combination is ideal as a conduit to getting in touch with
our deepest senses.

If you arrange to have the meal at home, you will have
more control over your environment and the food.
One of the ways you can both have fun and feel closer
is to share food from the same container. Any dish
that you cook in one container, whether a frying
pan, wok, or casserole dish will give you both the
opportunity to eat from the same pot. This is
common in Japanese cuisine where you use chopsticks
to share dishes like nabe.

The idea is that it will encourage you to interact,
and taking in the same food, with its chi energy,
means you have something in common in terms of
chi energy. This is why the traditional family meal is
such a good idea. When everyone sits down together
to share the same food, and energy, it creates a
bonding experience. If everyone eats separately, it can
create greater polarity.

Choose a suitable direction to sit with your lover.
This could be south to feel passion, west for
romance, southwest for a closer relationship, or
north for sexuality. Experiment and sit close to each
other so your chairs are at an angle, for example,
facing west and north.

Boost the energy
associated with romance
by placing red or pink
flowers in the west part
of your home or
bedroom. Red roses are
traditionally associated
with romance.

Keep the lighting low to make the mood intimate. Candles will keep the light focused on you and the table, and will give off a warmer, more orange hue. If you need additional lighting, use floor or table lights with low-wattage bulbs.

Red, pink, and purple will add excitement to your table setting. Use colorful, full-bloom flowers in these colors. Anything shiny will help spin the energy around your table a little faster, making the atmosphere more dynamic. This could be achieved with polished cutlery and fine crystal glasses. To balance this, use softer surfaces, such a linen table cloth.

If you want to make the room feel more intimate and relaxed, use a low, coffee table and sit on large cushions instead of chairs. This will make it easier to mess around with each other and have fun.

Meals where you share the same food give your energy fields something in common, making it easier for two people to feel closer.

Flaunt it!

The energy you surround yourself with in the form of clothes

will not only alter the way you feel but will also alter the emotions

of people close to you. Clothes are literally inside your energy field,

so they have a big impact on your mood. In addition, other

people pick up on the energy you are sending out.

Vintage silk underwear and a silk-covered bolster cushion printed all over with erotic images will add to the sensual ambience in a room dedicated to romance.

These mules have all the traditional elements of seduction: they're red, have a soft fluffy trim, and a satin high heel.

VITAL INGREDIENTS

The element water is associated with sexual vitality, mystery, and seduction in feng shui. It is an energy associated with the night and linked to a deep primal energy within us. Our bodies are, after all, 70 percent water and as an element it contains some of our deepest basic instincts. To increase this energy within your own aura use the colors cream or shiny black. Lace, silk, and sheer fabrics will further increase the presence of water chi energy around you. Anything loose and flowing will accentuate that watery feel.

A seductive red or pink is associated with the sunset to the west and the element metal. Bringing more of this energy into your personal energy field can make you feel more romantic, playful, and eager to enjoy the pleasures of life. It is interesting that the areas of a city concerned with sexual activities are known as the red light district. Similarly, the best geisha houses of Japan apparently had their entrance to the west and featured a red lantern hanging outside. Add more of this energy to your aura by wearing something with red or anything with metal, for instance, a red ribbon, red underwear, or red outer clothing. Metal jewelry or body piercing will increase the feelings associated with the west.

A bright purple or red color symbolizes both passion and excitement. This hot, fiery southern chi energy gets you noticed and projects a flamboyant image. It is excellent for feeling expressive and outgoing. It is ideal for parties and social occasions. Use these colors whenever you want to turn up these emotions. An item of clothing made of silk is also good for wearable seduction.

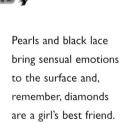

Pearls and black lace bring sensual emotions to the surface and, remember, diamonds are a girl's best friend.

Make space for sex!

Great sex is primarily made up of a feeling that you are almost as one; your bodies are entwined moving from one pose to another. Mixed in with this are all the sensations you take in of touch, sight, and sounds.

A group of lit candles creates low lighting in a bedroom. Bright lighting can make it too yang for sex. Place the candles in a safe position, away from where the action will be. They also add fiery, passionate energy!

To set up your bedroom for sexual pleasure you need to have the space to move and have the freedom to fully express yourself sexually. Having a large, soft bed helps. In addition, large cushions or a comfortable chair would help if you want to shift the action to other areas of your room.

Think about the kind of lighting to use in the room. You will probably enjoy looking at each other, so soft lighting is best. Candles are popular because they add more fiery, passionate energy to the room.

If you both love the touchy sensation of being close, a darker room will heighten these sensations. It helps if you can make the room soundproof so that you both feel uninhibited about the noises you might make while having great sex.

To create a more arousing atmosphere, bring sexual imagery into your room. For instance, sculptures of couples together, a painting, or photos of couples in erotic situations. Flowers such as orchids give off a scent that acts as an aphrodisiac, so a pair of orchids close to your bed will also help get you in the mood.

The energies to increase are water, fire, and western metal. These help you feel deeply sexual, passionate, and playful.

The water energy of the north is associated with sex and you can bring more of this into your bedroom with the colors cream and a shiny black. Lace and sheer materials will enhance this further. You could also hang a crystal in the north part of your room to enhance this energy.

People often find the feel of silk sheets, which represent fire chi energy, help them feel stimulated. You can also use bright purple, and red, to bring in more excitement and passion. Candles of similar colors will help further.

Pink flowers in a metal vase will bring in more playful western energy. The western part of your bedroom would also be a good place for any sexual or playful imagery. Experiment with some of these ideas and see how your sex life improves.

Above all, sex for wimps is fun! Get the sexual energy going by fooling around. These two had a lot of fun.

Nearly everyone is seeking sanctuary from life stress at the end of the day. This section contains four brilliant ideas for creating that sacred individual space.

Fix-its

Stress-busting

Ease into sanctuary

After a hard day the first thing you need to do is change your own chi energy so you can relax, unwind, and shake off the stress of the day. The easiest way to do this is to change the energy in the superficial energy field that surrounds your body.

Washing, taking a shower, or scrubbing your skin are quick ways to change your energy field, ideal for shedding the energy collected during the working day. Come home, chill out like a good wimp!

Taking off your work clothes when you get home will enable you to shed much of the energy you have absorbed during the day. To feel more free, wear loose, comfortable clothes around the home. Use natural fibers—cotton, linen, silk, or wool—so your chi energy field moves freely.

To change your energy more strongly, have a shower and wash yourself. The water will refresh and cleanse your outer energy field, helping you feel different. You can create a deeper change if you scrub your skin with a hot, damp cotton cloth, such as a small hand towel. Wring it out and scrub your body vigorously until it changes color all over. This action brings blood to the surface, making it easier to change its energy, which in turn will change your energy more deeply.

To change the energy of your home, open the windows for a few minutes once you get home to refresh the energy and make it easier to relax.

The more leafy green plants you have at home, the more natural the atmosphere will be. They will keep the energy alive and vital while you are at work, making it easier to feel you are in a sanctuary when at home.

When you want to unwind, choose to sit somewhere with plenty of space around you so your chi energy can disperse more easily. If the space is too confined, you may find your chi energy field becomes squashed and too intense. The calmest direction to face is north, so move the chair or couch to face that direction.

Leafy green plants keep energy alive and vital, especially when you work at home. Place the plants in convenient spaces, close to your energy fields.

Create calm

The colors in a room will change the light frequencies there and, as these pass through your own chi energy field, the light waves change your outer energy and make you feel different.

Choosing a color for a decorating scheme can be daunting, however, fabric suppliers and department stores provide an excellent fabric sample service, so it's easy to sit down with the samples and make an informed decision.

The yin colors will help make your home feel more calm. In general, these are pale and muted colors such as pale blue or green. In addition, cream is a gentle and calming color. Use these in your decorating scheme or simply add these colors to a room using accessories and flowers.

Flowers are an excellent way to bring color into a room as they also radiate a living energy, projecting the color more powerfully into the space around them. The gentle art of flower arranging is a calming process in itself. (Some of you wimps may not feel that way! But you can get the florist to do it for you.)

First think of the effect you want to create in that specific area of your home. Choose flowers that give off that kind of energy. For example, bright red roses will radiate a strong and vibrant yang energy, yellow daffodils will provide a fresh energy as they begin to bloom, and pink lilies will create an open, calming energy. Remember to change the water daily and trim the stems so that the flowers remain healthy.

To increase the natural calming energy of the space, place the plants in the north, northwest, or west part of the room, as these energies will help make the area feel easier to relax in. My preference would be to increase the energy of the north. In addition to putting your flower arrangement there, it would help to make sure the area is clean and uncluttered.

If you want to add more of a calming green color to a room, filling it with plenty of glossy foliage plants will be most effective. In a similar way to flowers, the plants will radiate their green color strongly as they also project their chi energy.

You can also bring more color to a room's decorating scheme by using paintings, hanging fabrics on the wall, and selecting natural fiber rugs for flooring. The advantage of all these ways to add color to a room is that they are easy to change, so if you feel the room has become too calming and needs more vitality, you can simply use more yang bright flowers in your next arrangement, or add a different cushion or rug. Make sure it's not wimpy!

Flower arrangements change the way you feel in a room and can be designed to suit your mood. This yin arrangement will help you to relax.

Get down!

When you have too many thoughts buzzing around it is hard to think clearly and get anything done. Sometime you just have to move your energy down to give your head the space to get some clarity again.

In this patio scene everything is placed low to the ground. Comfortable wire mesh stools have soft yin cushions covered with a pale fabric. All in all, this is a peaceful yin setting.

A quick way to bring the energy field to a lower level is to try to move some of your energy down to your feet. Soak your feet in hot, salty water for 10 minutes, and then dry them off vigorously with a soft towel, giving them a strong massage at the same time. This will increase the blood circulation in your feet, and make it easier for your chi energy to flow down there.

Another great idea to calm energy involves bringing the energy down in the room in which you want to relax. The easiest way to do this in the evening is to turn on only lights that are placed on the floor or on a low table. Overhead lights will stimulate energy higher in the room and, if close to your head, the brighter lighting will make it harder to calm down.

Lampshades of any shape or size will help direct the energy toward the floor. Cloth shades are more yin and can help to create a more relaxing atmosphere, although a metal shade can focus the light down more strongly. Another option would be to use candles, as these will generate a softer light in the space.

Sitting on low, comfortable chairs, sprawling on big cushions placed on the floor, or simply lying on the floor (on a soft rug) will help you center your energy better and feel more balanced.

Sitting on the floor, with a low coffee table to lean on, is a very good way to wind down after the day's activities. Natural materials add to the good vibes, as does the soft light created by candles.

LIGHTING

● Modern lighting designs feature low-wattage bulbs and dimmer switches to control the amount of light delivered, which are excellent for controlling mood.

● Choose lampshades made with natural fibers.

● The traditional paper lantern shade provides muted soft light for a calm ambience.

Make a water feature

Sounds can greatly help us relax as their sound waves vibrate the air passing through our own outer chi energy field. On hearing the sounds, our brains respond, helping to change our emotional state.

Equally you may be subjected to sounds that stir up your chi energy field and change your energy in a way that makes you feel irritable and tense.

One way to mask potentially stressful sounds is to create something called "white sound." This is a multifrequency sound, and what happens is that some of the sound waves will be opposite to the sound waves of the noise that stresses you, therefore canceling it out.

To my mind, the most natural and peaceful way to create a white sound is to use running water. Not only is the sound of running water relaxing, but it also creates a calming influence in the entire space.

Falling water will help bring the energy down, making it easier to feel settled. This is particularly influential since our bodies are mainly made of water and the chi energy of the water feature will interact easily with our own water chi energy.

It is important to keep the water fresh and clean so that it will have a beneficial effect on you. Dirty or stagnant water could have a negative influence. Change as much of the water as possible at least once a week. The advantage of a waterfall or fountain is that the process oxygenates the water, keeping it fresh longer.

Any water feature should be placed to the east or southeast part of your home so that it naturally enhances the type of energy in this part of your home. It will be more effective at improving the energy if you can put it somewhere that catches the morning sun as it rises in the sky.

You can buy ready-made water features, however, you may find it satisfying to make your own. Use natural materials, and change the water in it from time to time. This reactivates the energy.

1 Insert a water pump into a wide bowl. Cover the wire with decorative stones so it stays hidden.

2 Pour water into the bowl, covering the stones, filling it nearly to the top. Pile on more stones.

3

The sight and sound of gently
bubbling water is mesmerizing
and creates an aura of calm in
the room.

When it's all going well your career can be a huge source of inspiration and even give you more energy. In this section are five ideas for taking control and making the most of your career.

Fix-its

Work

Start a new career

To successfully start a new career you need enthusiasm,

confidence, and the belief that you can make it happen.

These qualities are found in the chi energy of the east.

To help you get off to the best start you need bring more eastern chi energy into your own chi energy field. The best way to increase the energy of the east in your home is to place a bowl in the east section. Refill the bowl each morning so that you bring more fresh water energy there. Water is supportive to the five element wood energy of the east and will increase the presence of this morning, springtime energy. This will be more powerful if you position the water so the morning sun hits it. You'll also enjoy the reflections dancing on the surface.

You can also increase the eastern energy by growing plants in the east—the plants represent wood energy and will bring more of that energy there.

Another effective way to absorb more eastern chi energy would be to work facing east, directly bringing this energy into your own chi energy field. If this is not possible try facing southeast.

Whenever you want to start something new, it is essential to clear the decks for action. This means getting rid of everything you no longer need, and making the space for something new to happen. Once you have the extra space, it is easier to feel you have the capacity to take on something new. It is much harder to start something when you are cramped for space and still surrounded by clutter from the previous projects.

1

Other wimps' clutter can be annoying when you are taking over someone's desk.

2

Sort through the remnants of office life and throw away whatever cannot be successfully recycled.

3

A clean, uncluttered working space will automatically make a good impression on superiors and colleagues.

Get promoted!

Getting a promotion is personally rewarding and it is an integral step in progressing your career. Taking in more of the energy that relates to leadership qualities will make it easier to reach your full potential.

The chi energy of the northwest is ideal for improving your chance of promotion. Its yang trigram of heaven associated with this energy represents taking control, being responsible, and acting with wisdom. Bringing more of this energy into your chi energy field will help you be perceived as having integrity, being trustworthy, and someone people will look up to.

To absorb more of this energy, place your chair and desk so you can work facing northwest. Remember to arrange this so that most of the room is in front of you, and you can see the door and windows easily. Sitting with your back to the rest of the room or general open-planned office is not a good move. You will not see who walks in when you are on the telephone, or how long they will stand there while you work. Who knows what they'll learn to your disadvantage!

You can increase the presence of northwestern energy in your office by placing a pendulum clock, with as many metal parts as possible, in the northwest part of your office work space or home-office area.

To bring more rhythm and structure into your work, it helps to have the rhythmic motion of a clock in your office. Interestingly, if you fill a room with pendulum clocks and set them off, they will all swing together after a while.

In addition, you can put more metal objects in the northwest part of your office, or even on the northwest part of your desk. An ergonomically designed metal-framed chair is an obvious accessory. So are metal pens and metal document trays. You can also wear metal objects. For example, a large, round metal watch will bring more northwestern chi energy inside your own energy field.

Experiment with some of these suggestions and see if you can work your way up the ladder.

Wearing a metal watch brings more metal chi energy into your personal energy field. This can make it easier to feel responsible and organized. A mechanical watch has more moving parts and will bring rhythm and movement into your energy.

The trigram of the northwest is associated with leadership, organization, and wisdom. Activating the metal energy of the northwest will enhance these qualities within you.

Set up a meeting

Meetings are all about good communication and setting up

a space so that people can express themselves effectively and

be heard. Be clear about what you want to achieve.

Is the meeting a free-thinking exchange to get new ideas, or a quiet meeting between two people to discuss a delicate issue?

When you want people to feel free to express themselves, interact, and be spontaneous, you need to set up the room so chi energy can move easily and people have the space to project their own chi energy field. It will help people express themselves better if you can see their whole body. It would therefore be better not to have any tables between people and keep work counters or equipment to the edges of the room.

Sitting on stools will help people feel more yang and interactive. If the stools are tall, it will also make it easier for the people at the meeting to stand up if this makes it easier to express themselves and use any communication aids such as flip charts. This up tree energy is ideal for being positive and moving the meeting forward.

When you need to have a settled meeting where the emphasis is on methodically getting through a task it would help to have more traditional seating and it would help to have a table. It is usually best to use a round or oval table for meetings so that everyone can see each other and interact easily. A round table symbolizes metal chi energy and helps contain the energy of the meeting around the table.

For meetings that require sensitivity it can help to use low, comfortable chairs. This will reduce the risk of someone getting overemotional. This kind of seating is good when you want people to feel relaxed and at ease. You can use a low table if you need work surfaces. This style will bring more soil energy into the room.

Sitting on low chairs is better for relaxed, contemplative meetings when you need to feel yin, patient, and calm. A yang tall chair is good for when you need to be quick, interactive, and dynamic. When one is in a higher chair than the other, this unbalances the power center. The taller person dominates, and the other person feels unsettled.

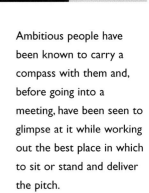

Ambitious people have been known to carry a compass with them and, before going into a meeting, have been seen to glimpse at it while working out the best place in which to sit or stand and deliver the pitch.

One-on-one meetings

You are all familiar with the feeling you get when you have an important meeting. Now is the time to throw off the wimplike attitude and go for it!

When having one-on-one meetings the relationship between the two of you will be influenced by the arrangement of chairs. This can greatly affect the outcome of the meeting, so it important to know what you want from the meeting. To make this easier, it helps to have a round table so you can take up different positions and combinations of directions.

When you arrange the chairs for a meeting, remember to look at the different directions you face using your compass, as this will also have an influence on how you both feel.

If you want to have a more confrontational meeting where you both need to be frank, honest, and to the point, it is better to be seated face-to-face. Here, you should arrange the chairs so they face each other. You will now meet each others' energy fields head-on and be able to pick up any little change in your colleague's expression. This would also be a better arrangement if you are trying to get a good deal from someone such as a supplier.

To create a more harmonious relationship, it would be better to arrange the chairs so you sit at an angle to each other. This still makes it easy to communicate and see each other, but your energy fields can merge, helping to reach agreement. I would use this for counseling, creative meetings, and generally relaxing with someone. You can sit closer together to try and reach greater harmony, or further apart if you think a little polarity would make your meeting more dynamic.

When you want to work closely with someone, it is better to face the same direction so you both absorb the same chi energy. You will find it is much easier to get on with the project and get things done. This arrangement is ideal for more practical, hands-on work where you do not want the confusion of lots of different ideas, or to be distracted by long discussions.

Sitting at an angle to each other helps both energy fields to merge in a harmonious way.

Sitting opposite each other is ideal for a frank, honest, and open meeting. There is no place to hide!

Sitting next to each other is helpful for teamwork. Here, your chi energy fields point you both in the same direction.

Feel the part

The clothes you wear, as well as your immediate surroundings, will have a big influence on the way you feel at work, so it is important to consider how to look and feel successful, and include the appropriate colors and materials within your energy field.

To get noticed, wear brighter colors, particularly touches of bright purple and red and, if you like patterned fabric, choose something with a star shape design. This will increase the fire energy around you, making you more visible. So, for men it's a plain red thick silk tie with a crisp white or blue shirt, and a sharp-edged suit; for women, it's a red suit or dress, red shoes, and a red handbag.

If you want to look and be more imaginative and creative, use a mix of colors. Include blue tones, but don't feel you have to coordinate anything. The more off-beat you make it, the more original your ideas will be.

Clothing with straight lines and sharp creases will help you appear more yang. Similarly, shiny shoes and fabrics with a sheen will speed up the energy around you and help you seem even more dynamic. You can add some bright colors to accentuate the yang energy further. This is ideal if you want to appear focused, quick-minded, and up to the task.

Metal accessories, such as a large watch, belt buckle, and jewelry, will bring more metal energy into your chi energy field helping you feel more dignified, responsible, and reliable.

Wearing bright white reflects energy away from you. White reflects all the light waves, helping you remain slightly aloof and apart from everything. This will help you stand out in a crowd, and is useful if you have a leadership role where you need to command respect from others.

Black has the opposite effect. It absorbs all the light waves, making it easier to absorb other people's energy, and feel closer to others. This is good when you want to create a team, and be able to tune into other people's mindsets easily.

This outfit is good for appearing friendly and a part of the team; for being seen as a fun person. However, it is unlikely to propel your career upward since you appear too yin to take on responsibilities.

This quirky outfit presents you as someone who is inventive, individual, and likely to have original thoughts at the whirl of a bright bow tie. The down side is that you may be seen as an outsider, and not one of the team.

TRY THIS

1   To appear ahead of the game, keep up to date. this is great fire energy.

2   To appear taller, increase the energy with vertical lines, sharp creases, and a jacket with a long line. Avoid horizontal lines, and cover belts and waistbands.

3   To get more respect at work, pay attention to every detail. Look immaculate. Enhance the metal energy within you.

4   On your first day at work, wear black. This increases soil energy and makes it easier for you to fit in with everybody.

In this section you'll find ways to increase your financial awareness and put you in charge of your finances. Feng shui details about selling, buying, or renting a home are also here.

Fix-its

Money matters

Money matters

Although money cannot buy you everything, it can go a long way to opening more opportunities in life. Apart from paying for the necessities of living, money can also be seen as representing appreciation and as a measure of what value people will put on something you have to offer.

The times when I have earned and saved the most money are the periods when I have generally relaxed about my finances. I know from experience that whenever you become worried, obsessive, or uptight about money, other people pick up on it and avoid you. It helps greatly if, regardless of your current financial state, you can create an atmosphere at home that is reassuring, and encourages you to think positively about your ability to bring money in.

It is unlikely that any amount of money will come from nowhere, regardless of how much you use feng shui to attract financial success. If feng shui could work this small miracle, all the feng shui practitioners would have retired by now! It is, therefore, important to have realistic means of bringing more money into your life.

Always make a point of keeping your options for receiving money open. When you least expect it, an exciting opportunity will come up from one of your options that has been quiet for a while. You might find it helps to have a few projects simmering away in the background of your everyday work that could turn into a new source of wealth. The more enjoyable the new source of wealth is, the more enthusiasm you will put into it, thus increasing your chances of success.

Do you need to feel more in control and organized about your finances (northwest) or need to cut back on spending and save more (southwest)? Find a convenient space to keep your banking details, checkbooks, and statements in the appropriate direction. Keep them neatly so everything is accessible and easy to use.

THE PRINCIPLES

The idea is that absorbing more of certain energies will help you get better at making money. First you will need to think what you need to change about yourself to increase your wealth. Do you need to be more focused on money, better organized, spend less, and save more or be more relaxed with money? Once you know what you need, use the suggestions below to bring a better atmosphere into your home. Remember to use the same direction in your home.

The chi energy of the west represents the fall and the harvest time. This is when you can focus on bringing things to a successful conclusion and reaping the benefits of your hard work. It is a useful energy when you want to get a little more for less work. As western energy is associated with metal, it is often linked to precious metals and wealth. Increasing this energy in your home can help you focus on ways to bring in more money.

The other metal energy of the northwest is particularly helpful when you want to be more organized with your finances. It is an energy that is associated with wisdom so, if you need to be more in control of your finances, it would be very helpful to increase this energy in your home.

Southwestern energy represents summer changing to fall and can be seen as similar to a squirrel storing its nuts for winter. This energy helps you make the most of what you have and is excellent when you want to save. It is the kind of energy that makes you feel you have achieved more at the end of a year than when you started.

Water energy, associated with the north, is also useful when you want to help money flow more easily. Flowing water can symbolize money moving through society.

10 TIPS
FOR BEING BETTER AT MAKING MONEY

1 Be clear on where the money will come from. For example, a promotion, raise, a part-time job, or investments.

2 Clean out, and keep tidy, the west, northeast, north, and southwest areas of your home.

3 Keep any cash, or your safe, in the west part of your home for greater income. Keep it in the south-west to save money.

4 If you have a fireplace, boiler, or oven in the west or northwest parts of your home, place some artist's charcoal in an earthenware pot as close to the fire as possible to harmonize the potentially destructive mix of energies.

5 Keep all invoices, statements, and other financial paperwork well organized and easily accessible. Review them so you feel aware and in control of what is going on in your financial world.

6 Grow money plants in the west, northwest and north parts of your home.

7 Avoid energy draining away from your home by fixing any leaking taps.

8 Reduce your exposure to stagnant water by getting rid of any mildew and dampness in and around your home.

9 Wear something that makes you feel good about money. This could be an item of jewelry, or a special watch.

10 Meditate from time to time on ways in which you could increase your wealth, and then relax about it. Becoming obsessive can make the situation worse.

Putting money in the west will help to increase your wealth. Try placing the largest denomination bill in your currency in the west part of your home. You can increase this energy by including a red, silver or gold ribbon, as this will accentuate the metal energy. Here, we used red-and-gold printed money envelopes.

Focus on wealth

Each part of your home has an influence on your ability to increase your wealth in different ways. The east will help you come up with new ways to earn money, the southeast to look at ways to increase your prosperity in the future and the northeast to be quick and seize the opportunity to make an investment.

Each of the eight directions listed gives you an idea on how a specific direction can help, and what to do in that part of your home.

Use the methods on pages 34 to 36 to find where the directions are, and then put the suggested items there. You can do them all, or just one of them. In addition, check which way the top of your head points when you sleep, as this helps you absorb more of that energy. For example, if you want to save money, sleep with your head pointing southwest.

EAST: place a moving water feature to help you start new money-making projects. Put a shiny coin into the water at the beginning of the day when you think you are on the verge of a breakthrough.

SOUTHEAST: put a bowl of fresh water on top of the largest bank note in your currency to increase your ability to get new ideas for future prosperity. Position it so the morning sun touches the water and refill the water as soon as you get up.

Yellow flowers increase the soil energy of the southwest associated with saving money.

Moving water represents vitality and moving through our planet in a similar way that money moves through society. Putting water in the southeast encourages you to be a part of the flow of money.

SOUTH: hang pictures of things that motivate you to earn more money. These are inspirational and keep you focused on the future.

SOUTHWEST: use a clay pot to keep your savings account details or simply keep a yellow flowering plant in a clay container to boost this energy.

WEST: shiny coins on a red cloth will increase this energy, making it easier to find ways to make more money out of what you are already doing. It also helps you have fun and enjoy making money.

NORTHWEST: keep financial information here if you want to get serious about your finances. Good for having more integrity about money and respect for the work that goes into earning it.

NORTH: hang a small, round, multifaceted crystal here to increase the energy that relates to your cash flow. Ideal if clients are slow paying you.

NORTHEAST: this is the winner's energy and great for quick decisions. If you like to speculate and play the stock market, increase this energy with a crystal.

Place the cloth and coins so they are easily visible. Shiny coins and a velvet, felt or silk cloth are ideal. Place a small round or oval mirror behind the coins to increase their influence.

Selling a property

When selling a property it is important to create an atmosphere that sells the house for you. The smell of coffee wafting through the air, of freshly baked bread, and spring air are all appealing.

The old adage that the smell of fresh coffee and baking bread will help sell a home is right. These kinds of smells will make people feel it is a healthy, happy home, and might even trigger an association with their own childhood homes.

As a seller you want every potential buyer to fall in love with the individual feel of your space, and sense that they, too, would be more than happy living there.

To achieve this, carry out a major spring cleaning and get rid of all the old energy, so that whenever someone comes around it feels fresh, clean, and ready to move into.

Try to get rid of as much as possible, even if this means putting things in storage for a while, so that your home looks as big as possible. It will even help to empty out cupboards so that people can easily imagine putting their own things in them.

If the decoration is looking a bit tired, and your home is not selling, try giving it a fresh coat of paint. White is the safest color, as it helps make your home appear slightly bigger, and makes the most of the natural light.

BUYING OR RENTING

The most important thing about buying or renting a home is to find out what happened to the people living there before. Ideally they will have had a good relationship, children, and financial success. Some homes will have a history of several families splitting up, or a run of people who have had financial troubles. These homes should be avoided unless you can see why this happened from a feng shui perspective, and you know how to remedy it.

Avoid moving into a home that is near electrical pylons, or an electrical substation as there is little you can do to overcome the potentially harmful electromagnetic fields. Similarly, living next to electric railway tracks, a nuclear power or processing plant, or anywhere exposed to toxic waste will be hazardous.

Look at the properties of the various directions on page 30 and decide which would help you most. See if you can find a home that faces this direction as more of this energy will enter your home. It is more practical to have a choice of several directions.

It is better to buy or rent a well-proportioned home with an almost square floor plan. This will make it easier to live a well-balanced life. An octagonal, or, if you want to be different, round floor plan will also be well balanced.

You should search for a home with good exposure to natural light and sunlight. In a city, this often means being higher up in a building so you are not in the shadow of other buildings. In rural areas, choose a home that has space around it.

Finally, make sure your prospective home is as natural as possible, especially if it is a new home, because many synthetic materials give off toxic fumes for years, filling your new home with unhealthy gases.

A fresh, clean atmosphere is important when selling a home. Opening windows, dusting everything, and making sure the floors are clean will help make a good impression.

Feng shui provides valuable insights into which colors,

materials, and objects to use in your home when you are

decorating so you can create the atmosphere you really want.

This section provides a few insights.

Decorate

it

Lighten up!

Lighting is unique in that you can quickly change the appearance and ambience of a room at the flick of a switch, or the glow of a candle flame. Good lighting makes people look their best at all times so it's a wise investment.

Candles give a soft orange hue of light, making a room feel warmer. The flickering of the candle light adds movement, too.

A contemporary Italian-designed table lamp casts a yin ambient glow onto the top of the console table.

By using a range of lighting in a room, you can change the mood from bright and lively to subdued and intimate to suit the appropriate occasion.

There are many ways in which you can harness the power of light to enhance a room. Uplighters are elegantly sophisticated and, as a design bonus, make a room appear taller and more spacious.

Spotlights pick out features in your room such as flower arrangements, paintings, sculptures, objets d'art, and plants. This type of lighting effect stimulates the flow of chi energy in a room.

For specific task lighting, fittings that use halogen bulbs are ideal because they generate a white light and that's crisp and clear.

Soft light from either table or floor lamps bring the energy down and generate a relaxing, intimate mood in a room. Your eyes are drawn down to the pools of light, and are not offended by glare. Colored light bulbs are great for that moment when you want to soften the atmosphere. There is a wide selection of colored bulbs available from most lighting stores.

Candles of all shapes and sizes, whether grouped on a ceramic platter, or placed in decorative glass candleholders, are the most yin and gentle light source in a room. They also create a restful and romantic ambience.

Use dimmer switches to keep the lighting scheme flexible and easy to control so you can quickly switch from one lighting theme to another.

Windows

Windows are the eyes of your home. Your friends and neighbors can tell a lot about you from the image you present to the neighborhood. So what's the best way to treat a window? Read on ...

A window allows you to see out from inside, and lets in natural light to each room. As a rule, large windows will help energy move through your home, while smaller windows make it easier to contain the energy in your home.

The ideal design is to have enough windows for good circulation of energy through your home, which can still contain the energy when you want to feel settled. The way to best do this is by using curtains or blinds to suit your room.

Curtains will create a softer, more comfortable yin atmosphere, whereas blinds encourage energy to move more quickly around the windows making your home feel yang and crisp.

With blinds, you have the choice of different materials and styles. The most yang would be metal, wood is neutral, and fabric is more yin. The choice of styles includes Roman, Austrian, Venetian, and roller blinds. Choose a style to suit the rest of your decor.

Whatever you use, it is good practice to set it up so you can expose as much of your window as possible. Window dressing that permanently covers some of the window will limit your ability to open up your home and get energy moving.

A simple curtain hanging from a natural wood pole is made more dramatic by the choice of color, design, and texture of the fabric. The partially closed curtain makes this room feel cozy.

Fabrications

Fabric is one of the most versatile decorating ingredients in the entire recipe for a decorating scheme. It comes plain, textured, multicolored, checked, striped, and blooming with flowers all over.

Adding fabric is another way in which you can lighten up a room. It's possible to change the look of a room by adding different and colorful cushions and curtains to the same background.

Large, plain blocks of bright color are the most yang, however, straight-line patterns such as stripes, checks, or a grid pattern also make a room more yang. Wavy lines or irregular forms break up the flow of energy, making it more yin.

The advantage of using cushions to bring color into a room is that you can play around with them, placing them in different parts of your room and trying out different combinations. Use bold colors if you are relying on the cushions to make a difference to the atmosphere of the room.

You can try using much stronger, bright yang colors for cushions as they mostly have a soft, matte, yin surface.

Choose a variety of colors and patterns so you can throw your cushions into different parts of the room to create a new feel.

Whoa!
Wimps can be
overwhelmed by a
myriad of colors,
shapes, and sizes of
cushions when making
decorating choices.

Floored!

From the moment you tentatively put your foot down on the floor in the morning you'll be walking on different types of flooring. Are they calming you down, or giving you the energy you need for the day?

Floors cover the largest surface area for which you have to choose a covering for in your home, and they are influential in defining ambience.

The most yang form of flooring is a hard, shiny, stone surface such as marble, granite, or concrete. Here, the chi energy picks up speed and moves freely. The space will feel energetic and be free from stagnation, but you may find it hard to feel relaxed in this environment. This is ideal for kitchens and bathrooms where it is best to keep energy moving.

Wood is a neutral surface and is suitable for most situations. It exudes the element tree in terms of chi energy, and creates an "up" feel in a space. Polished wood encourages energy to move quickly, while a rough, natural finish is better where you prefer to slow the energy. Use solid wood flooring rather than laminates, which may contain toxic bonding agents.

Use carpets where you want energy to slow down and you can feel comfortable, settled and relaxed. There is the risk that energy might move too slowly, leading to a stuffy, stagnant atmosphere. Use at least 80 percent wool carpets. Synthetic carpet carries a static charge of electricity which can irritate your energy field.

Wood floors with rugs are a flexible choice. Take up the rugs when you want to increase the flow of energy, and air them to reduce the presence of dust. Beating a carpet is good exercise!

The images illustrate the different ways energy flows. A hard marble surface makes it easier for energy to pick up speed, whereas a soft rug or carpet will slow it down. Wood is in between.

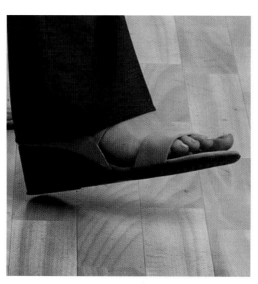

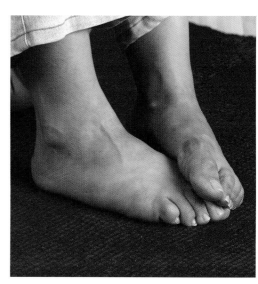

Furniture

Whatever you bring into your home will carry something of its own character. The painting by an inspired artist, the handmade rug, or the antique table will each have an energy of its own and, by putting the item close to places where you spend time, the object will, in a small way, influence you.

It is always better to have a few things that you really appreciate than surround yourself with a lot of possessions that do not reflect your life.

My preference is to find things that are as natural as possible and have a character of their own. As we have entered an age of mass-produced homes and furniture, it is too easy to create a synthetic and sterile living space by choosing the wrong items.

It is understandable that some people feel nervous about making design and decorating decisions. However, if you follow a few basic rules you can't go far wrong. It is important in feng shui to create an environment where you can look around a room and see shapes and designs that lift your spirits.

Having a variety of styles of furniture will provide a better balance in terms of yin and yang and the five elements. Tall furniture will increase the presence of that uplifting wood energy; spiky designs radiate fire energy; low, horizontal shapes, such as a coffee table, create a settled earthy feel; round shapes bring more metal energy, and wavy, flowing forms contribute more water energy.

Use freestanding furniture wherever possible so you always have the option to rearrange your room when it suits you.

The age of a piece of furniture will change the way you feel at home. If you desire a strong connection with your ancestors, keep some furniture they once owned, or those that remind you of them. You can re-cover them if they look a bit shabby.

A piece of modern furniture will bring more fresh, clean energy into your home.

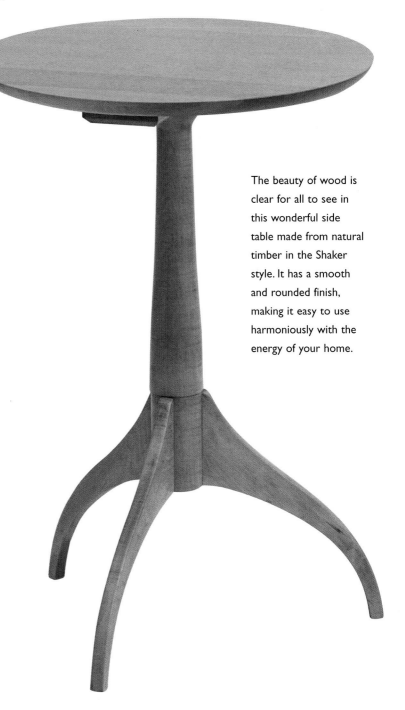

The beauty of wood is clear for all to see in this wonderful side table made from natural timber in the Shaker style. It has a smooth and rounded finish, making it easy to use harmoniously with the energy of your home.

Colors

Colors are an instant, powerful way to change your mood. Here, you will learn how to use color in your decorating scheme to not only make your home attractive, but to enhance your life.

The colors you use in your home will have a dramatic effect on its atmosphere. The colored surfaces will reflect certain light frequencies back into the room filling it with faster or slower frequencies depending on the color. These light frequencies will go through your outer chi energy field and change the way your energy moves. As a result, you will feel and think differently.

The brighter the color, the more yang and active it will make you feel. Bright reds, yellows, and oranges are good examples. Pale colors such as light blues and greens, will help you feel more yin and calm.

Before you decorate, think about how you want to feel in each room so you can choose the appropriate colors. Lay the transparency with the eight directions (page 41) over a plan of your home to see how the natural energies of each room will help you feel.

To find out how each color will make you feel look at the descriptions of the eight directions on page 30. Find a direction that has the properties you need more of and then see which color is associated with it. For example, if you want to feel more confident and assertive you would need more eastern energy in your chi energy field. The color that helps activate this energy is bright green. You therefore should find ways of including this color in your decoration.

To make it more powerful you can use the color in the same part of your home that its direction relates to. Lay the transparency over your plan to see which colors to use in different rooms. So, if you are using bright green, you would see if you could use it in a room in the east part of your home. Spending time in this room, particularly in the morning, will help you absorb eastern chi energy. I would try to include the colors of each direction in its most powerful place but you can use other colors with it. For example, you might have a white room in the east with just a touch of bright green.

When you are ready, paint large test patches on the wall and live with it for a few days to see how you feel. The stronger the color, the less you will need to change the energy of a room.

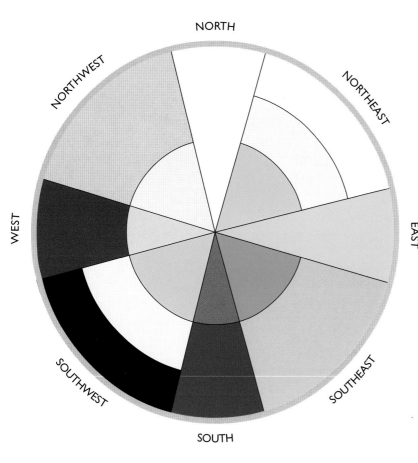

NORTH · NORTHWEST · NORTHEAST · WEST · EAST · SOUTHWEST · SOUTHEAST · SOUTH

The color wheel shows you the colors that are associated with each direction in your home. Decorating or placing something with a color from the chart in its appropriate direction will strengthen the natural energy.

The calming yin cream colors, associated with northern energy, are balanced by the touches of the yang bright red. Red picks up the energy of an otherwise peaceful room. You can see here you need only very small patches of a bright color to make a significant difference to a room.

Conclusion

Over the years that I have been using feng shui it has been a positive

force in my life, and I have been impressed by the way it has

helped other people. However, it is important to see it in context

and bring it into your life in a way that is empowering.

The art of feng shui is not set in stone and should be adapted to work for you . . . s**o don't be afraid to experiment**. Above all, approach it with a sense of humor! If you take it too seriously, you'll be too tense to **enjoy it** and make it a **positive force in your life**.

There are many ways you can use feng shui. This book has everything you need to start using it. There are many books that take the topic into greater depth. One area of confusion that frequently arises is that there are different styles of feng shui, some of them contradictory, so before you buy another book, check which style the author uses, and whether this is the area you want to learn more about.

I use a Japanese compass style. In other books, you can learn about how your date of birth can predicate you to certain directions, and how the date your home was built enables you to put a chart over a plan of your home, and superimpose another chart for the current year to get more information about your home.

The form school shows how to look at the shape of the landscape around you to see the way energy is moving. You can also learn more about the nine ki, or four pillar astrology, often used in feng shui.

Each version will add to your knowledge. However, too much too quickly can lead to being overwhelmed and lost in the subject. Study one aspect of feng shui at a time, and try it out before moving on to another branch. Taking a course in feng shui will certainly help you understand the topic and help to implement it in your life. Much will depend upon whom you study with, so use the following as a guide.

You may decide it would be easier to bring in a consultant and use his or her expertise to sort out the problems you think are present in your life and your home. Finding the right person is important, as you want someone with whom you feel comfortable, can talk to, and who has the knowledge and experience to genuinely assist you.

As with many unregulated professions, there is a wide discrepancy between people who have just read a few books and perhaps attended a few weekend courses and those who have professionally studied and have built up a respected track record. Ask questions and, if necessary, ask to see certificates to find out which type of feng shui practitioner he or she is.

Also, find out which style of feng shui they practice, and how long they have been working at it. Find out if he or she is a member of any professional organization, and if he or she follows a code of ethics.

Check to see if he or she has a professional liability insurance certificate and can provide you with a list of clients. The answers to these questions will show the degree of professionalism the consultant has.

Also, be clear on common sense things such as what the consultation covers, how much money is involved implementing the recommendations, and if it includes ongoing advice.

THE FENG SHUI NOVICES

Jowita Margola

A Polish girl with a popular personality, Jowita is a convert to the charms of feng shui. A student, she also works as a waitress and is now going to apply some of the work-related aspects of feng shui and see what happens!

Leo Bryan

Making a guest appearance in this book, Leo is heartened at the concept of good feng shui. He puts it into practice in meetings with office colleagues, especially when he wants to win an advantage point or two with ease.

Simon Lokko

An IT expert who travels the world, Simon was a cynic about the benefits of feng shui. However, the process must have worked, for during the shoot, he applied for and won a job in beautiful Switzerland.

Nina Roggero

An Argentinian among aliens during the World Cup football season, Nina needs no energy fix. Always bright and engaging, the team decided she was sleeping with her head the right way up from birth!

ACKNOWLEDGMENTS

Danielle, thank you for commissioning me to write the book. We survived all the FedExing! Maria, my sincere thanks for your styling contribution. Thanks to my darling D., my precious four boys, mum, my "little" bro. and his family, my big sis in Philadelphia and her tribe, my pals J.P., George, and Michael, and to all of you out there who were able to identify yourselves with the title of the book! And remember: You must not find symbols in everything you see. It makes life impossible. ENJOY!

The BookMaker would like to thank Asher office furniture (www.asher.co.uk); The Holding Company, The Chair Company (www.thechair.co.uk); Anna French Fabrics and Wallpapers, Shaker Furniture, Artemide GB Limited, Pennyfeather's of Hampstead, Lady Daphne of Chelsea, Mary for her inimitable design talent, and James and Amanda for the laughs.

Picture credits: 55, Elizabeth Whiting Associates; 88, Sanderson; 121, Zoffany fabrics.

Lucy Yallop
Straight after this shoot, Lucy traveled to Uganda to work on a newspaper, and spent a day or two with the Peace Corps seeing the country. Upon her return, it's back to university to finish her degree and graduate.

Barry Steele
Feng Shui was all words and a bit of confusion for Barry at the start of this shoot; however, by the end of it, he was seen buying a compass to check out which way his professional future was heading!

Jamie Fleming
If anyone is going to feng shui his loft, it's Jamie, who's been traveling for six months in South America and South Africa. An advertising copywriter by day, he relaxes by playing sports.

INDEX

A

accessories, decorating, **13**
acetate, **34**
acupuncture, **17**
animals, **15**, **28–9**
arguments, **13**, **62**
atmosphere, home, **12–13**

B

basements, **23**
bathrooms, **25**
bedrooms, **44–7**
  sexual pleasures, **80–1**
bells,**60**, **64**, **65**
blinds, **115**
body
  chakras, **14**
  meridians, **14**
boxes, **54–7**
buying houses, **110–11**

C

candles, **24**, **35**, **114**
  pairs of, **67**
  releasing stress, **88**
  romantic lighting, **71**, **77**, **80**
careers, new, **94–5**
ceilings, **18**
center, **33**
  finding, **39**
chakras, **14**
charcoal, **35**, **73**
chi energy, **16–17**
  definition, **14**
cleansing rituals, **62–3**
clearing up, **52–7**
clocks, **34**
clothes, **78–9**
  releasing stress, **85**
clutter, **52–7**, **62**
  workplace, **94–5**
coins, **35**
color
  clothes, **78–9**
  decoration, **120–1**
  releasing stress, **86**
compass, **34**
  using, **36**
confidence, **71**

contentment, **27**
control, regaining, **27**
corners, covering up, **58–61**
corridors, **23**
crystals, **35**
curtains, **115**
cushions, **116**

D

dancing, **65**
decoration, home, **12**, **112–21**
depression, **62**
directions, **15**, **30–3**
disorganization, **27**
doors, **18**
  bedrooms, **44**
dragon, **15**, **28**, **29**

E

east, **31**
  money matters, **108**
  new careers, **94**
  seating, **49**
  sleeping, **46**
  work position, **51**
eight directions, **15**, **30–3**
  floor plans, **40–1**
  relaxing position, **49–50**
  sleeping position, **46–7**
  working position, **50–1**
elements, **15**, **24–5**
emotions, **13**
  chi energy, **16–17**
energy, changing, **64–5**
equipment, **34–5**
erasers, **34**

F

fabrics, interior decoration, **116**
feet, soaking, **88**
feng shui, definition, **14**
fire, **15**
five animals, **15**, **28–9**
five elements, **15**, **24–5**
floor plans, **38**
flowers, **34**
  releasing stress, **86–7**
  romantic settings, **70**, **72**, **80**
Fu Hsi, **15**

furniture, **13**, **119**

G

glossary, **14–15**
graph paper, **34**

H

hand bells, **64**, **65**
health, **27**
houses, **12–13**
  atmosphere, **12–13**
  decorating, **112–21**
  selling, **110–11**
  vibes, **18–23**

I

ideas, chi energy, **16–17**
ignored, **26**
imagery, **66–7**
inflexibility, **27**

J

jumping, **65**

K

Kirilian photography, **14**

L

lighting, **23**, **35**, **114**
  corners, **60**
  lack of, **23**
  releasing stress, **88**
  romantic, **76–7**, **80**
loneliness, **26**

M

magic square, **15**
marker pencils, **34**
meals, romantic, **76–7**
measure tape, **34**
meditation, **64**
meetings, work, **98–9**
meridians, **14**
metal, **15**, **24–5**, **27**
mirrors, **23**, **29**, **35**, **59**, **70**, **71**
money, **27**
  financial matters, **106–11**
  saving, **26**
motivation, **27**

N

negative atmospheres, cleansing, **62–3**

north, **33**

  money matters, **108**

  seating, **49**

  sleeping, **47**

  work position, **51**

northeast, **33**

  money matters, **108**

  seating, **49**

  sleeping, **47**

  work position, **51**

northwest, **32**

  money matters, **107, 108**

  promotion, **96**

  seating, **49**

  sleeping, **47**

  work position, **51**

O

offices

  clutter, **94–5**

  meetings, **98–9**

P

pencils, **34**

phoenix, **15, 28**

photographs, **70**

pictures, **66–7**

plans, floor, **38**

plants, **34, 66**

  corners, **59, 60, 61**

  releasing stress, **85, 86**

promotion, **96–7**

property, selling, **110–11**

protractors, **34**

R

red cloth, **35**

relationships, **66–7, 69–81**

  clothes, **78–9**

  ending, **62**

  existing, **72–3**

  long-term, **26**

  moving closer, **74–5**

  romance, **76–7**

  space for sex, **80–1**

  starting new, **70–1**

  relaxing, **48–51**

renting houses, **110–11**

respect, **27**

romance, **76–7**

romantic feelings, **27, 70**

rulers, **34**

S

salt, **62**

scissors, **34**

sea salt, **34, 62**

seating, **48–51**

  meetings, **98**

sexual activities, **78–9, 80–1**

sexual vitality, **27**

sharp corners, **19**

shiatsu, **17**

sleep, **27**

  improving, **44–7**

  position, **30–3, 70, 71**

snake, **15, 29**

soil, **15, 24–5, 26**

sound, water features, **90–1**

sound waves, **60**

south, **31**

  money matters, **108**

  relationships, **71**

  seating, **49**

  sleeping, **46**

  work position, **51**

southeast, **31**

  money matters, **108**

  relationships, **71**

  seating, **49**

  sleeping, **46**

  work position, **51**

southwest, **32**

  money matters, **107, 108**

  relationships, **72–3**

  sleeping, **46**

  work position, **51**

spring cleaning, **52–7**

stairs, **18**

storage, **54–7**

  bedrooms, **44**

stress, **82–90**

sun, directions, **37**

sunsets, **15**

T

tiger, **15, 28, 29**

trigrams, **15**

tools, **34–5**

tortoise, **15, 28**

tree, **15, 24–5, 26**

W

walls, **28–9**

washing, releasing stress, **84, 85**

water, **14, 15, 24–5, 27**

  money matters, **107, 108**

  sexual vitality, **79, 80**

  water features, **34, 90–1**

wealth, **108–9**

west, **32**

  money matters, **107, 108**

  relationships, **70**

  seating, **49**

  sleeping, **47**

  work position, **51**

wind chimes, **24, 34**

windows, **18**

  bedrooms, **44**

  decorating, **115**

withdrawn, **26**

wood, **24–5, 26**

work, **92–103**

  meetings, **98–9**

  new careers, **94–5**

  promotion, **96–7**

  seating position, **50 –1**

Y

yin and yang, **15**